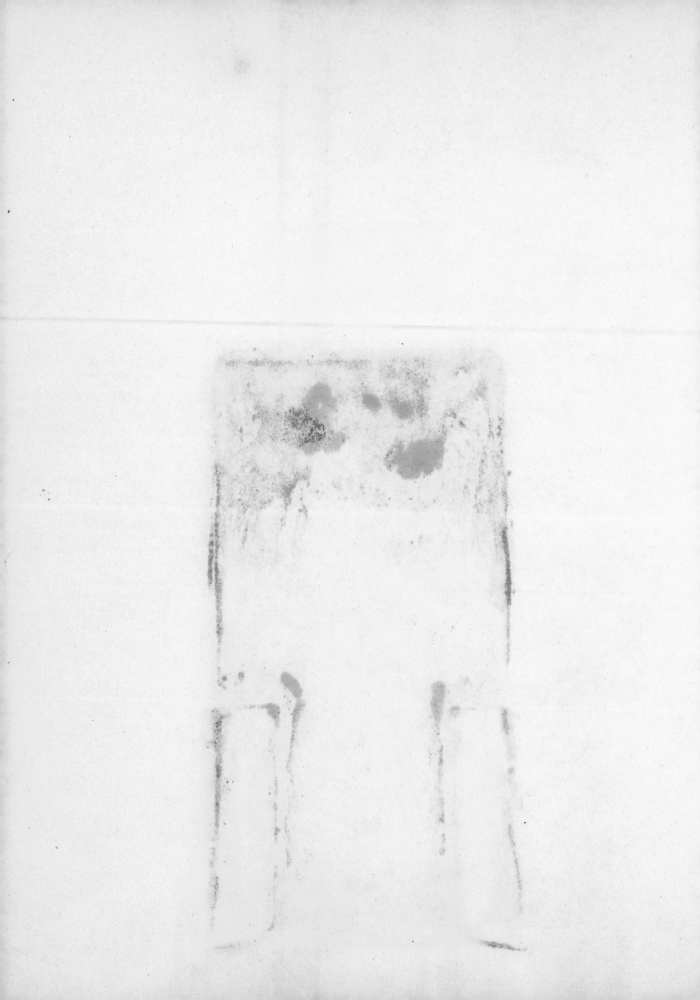

THE VIEW FROM RED SQUARE

Dedicated to the Memory of

Dr. Darinka M. Milenković

and

Margaret Calhoun Duff

THE VIEW FROM RED SQUARE

A CRITIQUE OF CARTOONS FROM
PRAVDA AND IZVESTIA, 1947-1964

BY

Michael M. Milenkovitch, Ph.D.

Department of Political Science
Hunter College

HOBBS, DORMAN & COMPANY, INC. — PUBLISHERS
New York   Buenos Aires

PREFACE

Since the end of the Second World War the United States and the Western Allies have secured their existence through powerful military alliances. These ties have remained steadfast despite growing differences of opinion. Now we have reached a stage that will be characterized by increasing individualism on the part of many nations. These changes are related to the changing nature of the Cold War and its transformation from a series of armed conflicts to a prolonged era of "peaceful coexistence" and active economic and ideological competition.

The implications of such a shift in locus are great. The disparity between efforts in the ideological competition—the propaganda gap —may prove as dangerous to the West as the missile or sputnik gaps appeared to be in the recent past. The propaganda gap is all the more dangerous as its impact and results are less visible. Its damage is far more difficult to repair, since it is in the minds of people strewn all over the world who cannot be reached in a simple manner because of their various languages, cultures, social, and religious beliefs.

This study of one specific aspect of Soviet propaganda activities is designed to enhance our understanding of Soviet propaganda techniques. These techniques are used to manipulate minds—in this case those of the Soviet people—to use their desire for peace in order to lead them along a road of hate and distrust and ultimately to intensify tension at home and abroad, endangering that peace which their propaganda ostensibly upholds.

The focus of this study is the image of the outside world presented to the Soviet readers through the cartoons of the two leading Soviet papers, *Pravda* and *Izvestia*. Special attention is paid to Soviet interpretations of various aspects of the Cold War and to the presentation of the West—chiefly the United States—to Soviet readers.

The cartoon is a valuable indicator of this image because of its impact (as a visual and written message) and for ease in identifying clearly the themes and symbols contained within it. Further, since all Soviet information flows from a central propaganda machine, the cartoon reflects the overall content of Soviet propaganda.

Presented here is a selection of 120 cartoons that appeared in *Pravda* and *Izvestia* during the past seventeen years. The first thirty-four cartoons are representative of twelve years of the Cold War (1947–1958), while the remaining eighty-six span the six years, 1959–1964. The work of some twenty Soviet cartoonists is represented. Two eras—Stalin's post-war years, and Khrushchev—are examined and contrasted.

If the reader is either aroused or bored by these cartoons, he should try to envision his reaction in relation to the time of their appearance in the Soviet press. It is hazardous to guess how Soviet readers feel when viewing this sinister gallery of images, but depending on the level of sophistication, the response must either be anger at the warmongers or utter boredom with the constant repetition of some thirty basic themes.

Part One of this study of Soviet cartoons provides an introduction to the theory, organization, and make-up of the Soviet newspaper, as well as a discussion of the Soviet cartoon itself, to specify the role of the cartoon in the Soviet communication process.

Part Two is descriptive and analytical. It examines in detail the Soviet view of the West as shown through cartoons both as domestic mirrors of Soviet foreign policy and as instruments in the perpetuation of the propaganda Cold War.

Part Three summarizes the new look in Soviet cartoons, and relates the flow of cartoons over the years to Soviet foreign policy.

Gratitude and thanks for encouragement to undertake this effort are expressed to Professor Michael T. Florinsky of Columbia University; also to Professors Quincy Wright and John N. Hazard for support and guidance in shaping some parts of this book while the author was a student at Columbia.

Thanks are also given to Walter E. Hering and to the staff of the Slavic Acquisitions Department of Columbia University Library for assistance in assembling the cartoon materials and reproducing the materials on which this book is based.

Editorial assistance and perception of some of the more salient aspects of this investigation were offered by my Columbia classmate, William I. Stewart; my colleague at Hunter College, John W. McDonald, Jr.; and my wife, Deborah. However, the author assumes responsibility for all statements and conclusions with the hope that this work will illuminate one aspect of the Soviet propaganda assault against the West.

MICHAEL M. MILENKOVITCH

Hunter College
City University of New York
New York, 1966

CONTENTS

PART THREE   SOVIET PROPAGANDA POLICIES IN THE COLD WAR

PART ONE

THE SOVIET NEWSPAPER
AS A PROPAGANDA WEAPON

Words and pictures have played a more continuous, and perhaps a more vital role than bullets or rubles in Moscow's struggle to undermine the social order of capitalism and to reconstruct society on "Marxist-Leninist" foundations.

FREDERICK C. BARGHOORN
(Soviet Foreign Propaganda, Princeton, 1964).

CHAPTER ONE

THE POLITICAL CARTOON

AND INTERNATIONAL TENSION

The intent of this case study is to survey the Soviet use of the cartoon media since the introduction of the Marshall Plan in mid-1947. Its primary source is the cartoon as it appeared in the two leading Soviet newspapers, *Pravda* and *Izvestia*. The cartoon, by its very nature, is a persuasive device. While it is difficult to repeat the written word or banner headline a few days after its appearance, the impact of an arresting cartoon may linger much longer.

The cartoon may be especially potent in a dictatorial society where the state controls and coordinates all means of communication: the printed media—newspapers, magazines, and books; the audio and visual media—radio, films, and television. The messages of the component media may be coordinated to produce a single monolithic image of the rightness of a country's policy; the message may be fortified, through repetition. There is no differing point of view which can detract from the one presented from above. In an "open" society, with its multiplicity of viewpoints and opportunities for their expression, it is much more difficult to mobilize the entire population for a single course of action, in either domestic or foreign policy. In the "closed" society there is no source voicing opposition to the policies of the regime.

There are varying degrees of dictatorship, with corresponding implications for the press. The traditional dictatorship of Franco's Spain does not compare to the totalitarian dictatorships of Hitler or Stalin in extensiveness of power. The traditional dictatorship *censors* the press, whereas the totalitarian regime *dictates* every move. The action of traditional dictatorships is negative toward the press, restraining and preventing. The dynamic totalitarian dictatorship is positive with respect to the press, restlessly ordering and directing. The Soviet totalitarian dictatorship has had the additional advantage of being able to insulate its people more effectively from external sources of information than could the Central or Western European countries.

In the past, dictatorships and aggressive countries have often prepared their populations in advance for oncoming conflict or war by constructing, over longer or shorter periods of time, a diabolical image of the opponent. The use of the press to inflame passions in such a manner was evident in Central Europe at the turn of the century and perhaps contributed to the outbreak of

3

World War I. Propaganda reached a peak in the European dictatorships before the outbreak of World War II. As a prelude to armed conflict, Nazi Germany during the thirties painted a sinister portrait of Bolshevik Russia. For its part, the Soviet Union and the international communist movement followed suit with a damnation of fascism and of the entire capitalist West, until the latter policy was temporarily abandoned in the interest of constructing "popular fronts" against Hitler——temporarily, because the Soviet Union resumed its jagged portrayal of the West and the United States following World War II, intensifying it at times to near hysteria.

Even if the Soviet press and its cartoons were being utilized solely to divert popular attention from internal difficulties, the West can neither overlook nor regard lightly the possible consequences. If only for this reason, one should study Soviet political propaganda to see if an ominous parallel appears.

Propaganda, in common parlance, is the dissemination through mass media of doctrines, political theories, specific interpretations of events, and explanations of policies designed for mass public consumption. In the Soviet Union, where propaganda is a fine art, a distinction is made between "propaganda" and "agitation." "Propaganda" refers to the dissemination of a broader body of ideas in their more profound content and thorough elucidation among a comparatively narrower circle of people. "Agitation" is exercise of political influence over the masses by means of talks, reports, speeches, through newspapers, books, brochures, leaflets, the radio, and motion pictures. It operates on a mass scale and disseminates among the masses a body of ideas and knowledge narrower in scope and content than "propaganda."[1]

This study of Soviet propaganda through cartoons seeks several answers.[2]

What is the image of the West projected by the Soviet press in its cartoons of the Cold War? Is that image becoming more belligerent, nationalistic, and expansionistic? Does it stimulate fear within the Soviet Union of the "danger" represented by the West? What have been the specific responses in cartoons to events of international and Soviet domestic significance, and what do these reveal about Soviet motivations in conducting the Cold War?

To answer these questions, seventeen years of Soviet cartoons have been surveyed, years which included developments of the Cold War ranging from extreme tensions to relative relaxation: the Marshall Plan, 1947; the Berlin blockade and the anti-Tito campaign, 1948–1949; commencement of the Korean conflict, 1950; the truce talks and armistice, 1951–1953; the death of Stalin, 1953; the Foreign Ministers' Conference, 1954; the Geneva Summit Conference, 1955; the Hungarian-Suez crises, 1956; the resolution of the Soviet succession problem and the rise of Khrushchev, 1957; the Middle East and second Berlin crises, 1958; Khrushchev's visit to the United States and the ensuing "spirit of Camp David," 1959; the U-2 plane incident, the Paris Summit Conference, and Khrushchev's second trip to the United States for the United Nations General Assembly Session, 1960; the Berlin Wall, Cuba, the Congo, Laos, the Kennedy-Khrushchev meeting, 1961; the Cuban missile confrontation, 1962; the nuclear test ban treaty and the assassination of President Kennedy, 1963; international dissension within the Eastern and Western alliances, progressive chaos in Southeast Asia, and the sudden and dramatic fall of Khrushchev, 1964.

In order to evaluate the significance of Soviet cartoons during the last seventeen years, it is necessary to have a framework within which to view them. The framework consists in part of the outlines of the Cold War and the developing tensions between the superpowers. In part it consists of changes in the Soviet domestic scene that have been a part of Soviet life since the death of Stalin in 1953. These changes have affected the position and usage of the propaganda process, and specifically of the press and the cartoon, as well as the formulation of general Soviet foreign policy objectives.

It is possible to identify three phases of the Cold War since 1947. (Since this review starts in 1947, the take-over of Eastern Europe is not included, as the conditions for its accomplishment were virtually completed by 1947). Zhdanov's speech of September, 1947, at the opening session of the Cominform (Communist Information Bureau) that declared the division of the world into two hostile camps could be taken as the Soviet acknowledgement of the Cold War.[3]

The first phase extended from 1947 to the death of Stalin in March, 1953, which "marked the end of an era and opened the way for a new constellation of power to emerge."[4] This phase was characterized by a limited offensive: the Berlin blockade of 1948–1949 and the Soviet approach to the Korean War exemplify this policy. In both cases the limits of Soviet aggression appear to have been defined by a recognition of the disparity between the total power of the Soviet bloc and that of the United States. At the time of the Berlin blockade, the United States had a nuclear monopoly. (Although the Soviet Union exploded its first atomic bomb in September, 1949, it could not have developed a nuclear striking force for some years after.) In both cases, due in part to this disparity, the Soviet Union did not press its objectives so far as to entail involvement in more than a local war. Thus the Berlin blockade was ultimately broken, and the Soviet Union refrained from direct involvement in the Korean War.

The second phase, 1953–1957, was characterized by the struggle for succession. Immediately after Stalin's death came the short-lived triumvirate of Malenkov, Beria, and Molotov. Beria was shot, Malenkov was dismissed after two years as Premier and replaced by Bulganin. The struggle finally culminated in July, 1957, when the "anti-party group," including Molotov, Malenkov, and Kaganovich, was purged by Khrushchev, with the support of Marshal Zhukov of the Soviet Army. Marshal Zhukov was purged from leadership shortly thereafter, in October, 1957.

This struggle occurred within a framework of de-Stalinization in both internal and external policy. Examples of the internal changes were the curbing of the power of the secret police and closing of Soviet forced labor camps; and in foreign policy, reversal of the isolationism of Stalin was visible in the numerous trips abroad by Soviet leaders (to India, Burma, and Afghanistan) and in the reconciliation with Marshal Tito. This international change of mood was illustrated by the Indo-China armistice of 1954, the signing of the Austrian treaty in May, 1955, and the Summit Conference of July, 1955, that was characterized by the "spirit of Geneva." In May, 1955, however, the Warsaw Pact joining the East European countries in a military alliance came into existence. The continuing struggles within the Soviet leadership apparently prevented the emergence of a single strong leader and a single strong policy. The foreign policy pursued in this period was almost one of caution and conciliation. The problems in East Europe during 1956, the Polish October, and the Hungarian November uprising, did not in themselves seem to have had a marked effect on Soviet policy vis-à-vis the West; but these events did preoccupy the Soviet leaders and required the concentration of their attention.

The third phase, the rise and fall of Khrushchev, might be dated from the second half of 1957 to October 15, 1964. It began with the consolidation of Khrushchev's power after the ouster of the "anti-party group," and with the increase in general Soviet confidence and morale after the technological feat of Sputnik I in October, 1957. "Once the succession crisis had been resolved by Khrushchev's purge of his competitors, the outlines of a new model of totalitarianism began to crystallize."[5]

After 1957, when Stalin's successors, emboldened by missile and space achievements, began to claim that the balance of power was shifting in the Soviet favor, peaceful coexistence began to reveal its offensive potentialities.[6]

The years from 1958 to 1964, the Khrushchev era, were marked by a change in the character of the hostility between the Soviet Union and the West, in comparison with the years 1953–1957. This hostility differed from that of the post-war Stalinist era in at least two major respects: (1) The Soviet Union had, or felt that it had, more power than before with which to support its more offensive stance. With the development of ICBM's, an atomic arsenal, and other technical advances, the Soviet Union had what previously was lacking —the capacity to reach the mainland of the United States. (2) At the same time, however, came (it is generally believed) a clearer awareness of the destruction that could result from a nuclear war and for this reason, among others, emphasis upon themes of peaceful coexistence and a shift in the focus of the Cold War to the diplomatic, ideological, and economic arenas. This shift was attended by an extension of the areas of Soviet engagement from the periphery of the Soviet Union and China (Eastern Europe, Korea) further into Southeast Asia (Laos, South Vietnam), Latin America (Cuba), Africa (the Congo, Guinea, Ghana), and the Middle East (Iraq, Yemen, Egypt). These areas at times enjoyed support through increased foreign aid, provision of military and technical advisers, and of military and technical equipment. On the other hand, the Soviet Union frequently flexed its military muscles and rattled rockets before the eyes of the world.

Khrushchev's threat, in response to the 1961 Bay of Pigs invasion of Cuba, to counter with ICBM's capable of reaching the American mainland, is well known. Other threats were extended to countries with U-2 bases, and to those belonging to NATO or other Western alliances. The Greeks were understandably excited by Khrushchev's remark that "not even the Acropolis" would be spared. The British replied to such threats by sending blueprints of the retaliatory capability of their nuclear striking force. During this period Berlin continued to be an area of contention between East and West.

The Cold War has had many facets and has affected the entire face of the world since its inception almost two decades ago. Many weapons have been employed by the Soviet Union in waging this intense conflict. One such weapon, the cartoon, continues to play a special role in this conflict. The political cartoon, a humorous but subliminal persuader of the human mind, can contribute to the enlistment of support for government policies, even those which are suicidal. This includes a policy which, in its determination to carry the new Eastern imperialism around the world, might destroy the earth itself. This underscores the importance of the study of the political cartoon, one aspect of the opponent's centrally planned communications apparatus.

CHAPTER TWO

THE SOVIET PRESS

Publishing enterprises must not be permitted to abuse their autonomy by pursuing a policy that is not entirely the Party policy.

V. I. LENIN[1]

The press is the sharpest and most powerful weapon of our Party.

J. V. STALIN[2]

The press is a chief ideological weapon of the Party. It is called on to smite the enemies of the working people. As the army cannot win without waging war, so the Party cannot carry on its ideological work without such a sharp and fighting weapon as the press.

N. S. KHRUSHCHEV[3]

The Soviet information system as a whole and, hence, the Soviet newspaper differs essentially from that of the West. The press is controlled by the Party, is utilized for specific ends, and uses certain means to attain these objectives.[4] The most striking difference between the two systems is the absolute control of all printed matter by the state:

A citizen may not . . . so much as operate a mimeograph or duplicating machine for the publication of handbills. He may not use the printed word to spread his ideas, except through channels provided by the state.

Even state-operated printshops are censored under a law requiring submission prior to publication, of all matter prepared for reproduction . . .

Public opinion can be effectively expressed only through a licensed agency.[5]

ORGANIZATION OF THE SOVIET PRESS

Unlike the United States, there are in the Soviet Union and in Western Europe nation-wide newspapers circulated throughout the country and published simultaneously in several cities. The two leading Soviet papers circulated nationally are *Pravda* and *Izvestia*.[6]

Most influential in the Soviet Union, with by far the largest circulation (and among the largest in the world), is Moscow *Pravda*. It is the organ of the Central Committee of the Communist Party of the Soviet Union and is published daily in over six million copies.[7] *Pravda* is printed simultaneously in twenty-two cities from matrices flown from Moscow throughout the entire Soviet Union. It is the official daily source of information and interpretation of all events considered relevant by the Party.

Moscow *Izvestia,* the organ of the Presidium of the Supreme Soviet of the Soviet Union, is the second most important newspaper distributed nationally. In addition to presenting essentially the same news and interpretation as *Pravda,* it carries lengthy government decrees but less Party news, which is primarily the responsibility of *Pravda.* This is in accord with two decrees of the Central Committee of the Communist Party of the Soviet Union, which called for a division of tasks between the two papers.[8] Both carry more international news than do other Soviet newspapers, most frequently in the form of identical TASS or APN dispatches or stories written by their respective correspondents abroad. During the editorship of Aleksei Adzhubei, Khrushchev's son-in-law, *Izvestia* developed a more interesting news presentation. Its stories were less dry and more readable, and occasionally it carried interviews or texts of statements by Western leaders. The best-known example was Adzhubei's interview with President Kennedy on November 29, 1961. *Izvestia* is published simultaneously in eighteen cities 300 times a year, and its circulation according to 1961 figures was 4.1 million;[9] but according to Mr. Adzhubei during his visit to the United States in November, 1961, its circulation was over five million.[10]

CONTROL AND ADMINISTRATION
OF THE SOVIET PRESS

There are four different channels of control.[11] (1) Administrative control through the organizational structure of the press. Such organizations as the Party, government, trade union, army, have their own papers, often at several levels. These publications are subject to administrative control through their own organizations. (2) Administrative control through government channels (allocation of paper, circulation). (3) Administrative control through party channels. After 1939, the Department of Agitation and Propaganda of the Central Committee of the CPSU controlled propaganda and agitation activities.[12] The exact methods of control of the press by the Party were not specified.

However, from the great bulk of its published decrees concerning the press, a pattern of control becomes clear. It is composed of these elements: first, the force of its substantive decrees—those conveying specific editorial directions, prohibitions and reprimands; second, suppression and review of the press by Party organs; third, close involvement of the Party machinery at all levels in the operation of the press; and fourth, detailed attention by the Party to the personnel of the press, including the training and selection of editors.[13]

(4) Administrative control through inter-press review. Central newspapers exercise vertical control by publishing periodic reviews to point out general or specific deficiencies.[14] "The supervision achieved through 'inter-press review' gives the press control system its final touch of ubiquity."[15] A recent Soviet publication on the press confirms these observations.[16]

In article 36, part IV of the Statutes adopted at the Nineteenth Congress of the Party, it is stated: "The Central Committee of the Communist Party of the Soviet Union . . . appoints the editorial boards of the central organs working under its control, and appoints the editorial boards of party organs of large city organizations."

That does not mean that the Central Committee of the CPSU appoints the personnel of the central organs of the press. It appoints the leading workers of the newspapers: the chief editor, his assistants, the secretary of the editorial office, editors of chief departments. Other personnel are selected by the editorial boards of the central newspapers and journals.

The Central Committees of the Communist Parties of the Soviet Republics, regional and local committees appoint the editorial boards of the Republic, regional, and local organs working under their control; the city and *raion* committees of the party appoint the editors of the city and *raion* party organs; plant, factory, higher schools, and other party committees appoint the editors of the plant, factory, and higher school newspapers.[17]

Nor does the influence of the party end with making the appointments:

> For the successful performance of newspapers, journals and other organs of the press it is very important that their managers be very closely associated with the Party committees, be in touch with activities which convey to them the well-known concrete tasks that face the republic, region, district, city, or *raion* at a given time. Without such conditions there is an unavoidable loss of contact with life, loss of contact with the actual tasks of the present day.[18]
>
> Specifically, the editor is continually in contact with the party committee of which the newspaper is the organ. He participates in its activities, in the work of the conferences, plenums, meetings of the *aktiv,* and is obliged to be in the midst of the activities of the party organization. All this is necessary for him to direct successfully the work of the editorial office.[19]

The editor is required to read and give approval to each newspaper column; to appraise the quality and content of every article, illustration, or report that goes into the newspaper; and to give attention to the layout.[20] The editor is solely responsible as manager. For example, the editor of *Vecherniaia Moskva,* A. A. Fomichev, was dismissed in November, 1959, after being severely criticized for not playing as his lead story the successful Soviet space shot, but instead featuring an item of local interest.

The editor carries out his work in conjunction with the editorial board whose advice he seeks on the management of the newspaper.[21]

As in most other aspects of Soviet life, planning is essential:

> The successful work of the editorial board is impossible without a clear perspective and operative plan.
>
> The Central Committee of the Party repeatedly has emphasized that the plans of the editorial of-

fices of the newspapers and journals must be approved in agreement with the Party committee. That enables the editorial office to coordinate its actions with the Party committee, to work together with their directives.[22]

Khrushchev commented upon the importance of forethought:

> One must work with a newspaper intelligently and not prepare it the same day that it will be put to press. The editor must foresee not only the theme, but also select a competent journalist who can prepare this theme in such a manner that the readers, like a person after a good meal, would desire to lick their fingers after finishing.[23]

There are different forms of planning. The general plan of the editorial board is composed for a period of several months and determines the general character of the paper. It gives directives to the departments specifying the basic, most important themes. The plans for the departments are further subdivided, and individual tasks are assigned.[24] The long-range plan can forsee only the basic themes. On the basis of this plan, however, the general monthly plan is worked out. "In it concrete themes, subjects, authors, and the date for setting the material into type are indicated."[25]

Not only is there a long-range plan for the content of the newspaper, but its approach to presenting the day-to-day news is quite at variance with Western practice. Soviet discussions of the role of news information make it clear that only selected items of information are suitable for publication.

> News information is agitation with the help of facts. While selecting the purpose of information, the author of the information report must always take into account that not all happenings should be reported in the pages of the paper. In this capacity the *purpose of information* must be to select facts and events which will serve to ease the problems which face the Soviet peoples in their tasks of building communism.[26]

The role of the journalist has been defined. Khrushchev has told Soviet journalists in an address to the Congress of Soviet Journalists that they are "not only official subordinates, but literally assistants of our Party—the active participants for a great cause [stormy applause]. Why assistants? Because you are the permanently available active voice of the Party. Whenever some decision ought to be explained and implemented, we call upon you, and you, like the most faithful driving belt, take the Party's decisions and carry them into the midst of our people [prolonged applause]."[27]

The primary purposes of the paper are to arouse support for government policy, to mobilize the masses, to generate enthusiasm for mastering the tasks posed by the Communist Party. Responsible Western journalism concentrates its efforts on the function of informing, especially in news and pictorial reporting, and much less on persuasion.

> The Soviet press is predominantly an instrument for communication going from the party and government to the people and the public organization of the nation. The newspaper is a device through which the party and government transmit decrees and decisions, in which they present, explain, and justify their policies. Throughout all the material, domestic and foreign, there runs a constant theme of greater exhortation for greater effort and sacrifice, and for firmer support of the authorities. . . . The rest is a kind of house organ of the party and government units at all levels.[28]

The significance that Soviet leaders attach to control of the communication media was strikingly illustrated following Khrushchev's removal. Almost immediately the Chairman of the State Committee for Broadcasting and Television, Mikhail Kharlamov, as well as Aleksei Adzhubei of *Izvestia,* and other top-ranking personnel, were replaced. A month later the dismissal of Pavel A. Satiukov of *Pravda* was revealed.

SKETCH OF A SOVIET NEWSPAPER

The typical Soviet newspaper, like most European newspapers, is smaller than its American counterpart. Paper for news is not allocated by the planners in large quantities, and most Soviet papers carry little advertising. Soviet papers have four to sixteen pages, with additional pages in the Sunday editions. The front page usually carries one large picture, often of the Party leaders, of members of the working class singled out for praise, or of popular demonstrations in support of Soviet domestic and foreign policy. The editorials appear in the first two columns on the left side of the front page to distinguish them from the news. They are considered official statements and explanations of Party policy. Stories on internal developments, TASS bulletins, telegrams from workers' delegations, and news stories similar to those familiar to the Western reader appear. The print used throughout the papers is larger than in most Western papers, resulting in fewer words in an equivalent amount of space.

Foreign news is received from the TASS agency (Telegraph Agency of the Soviet Union)[29] and its correspondents, from APN (Novosti)[30], and from the permanent correspondents of *Pravda* and *Izvestia* scattered throughout the major world capitals. A third source of foreign information is comment and news critical of the West appearing in the Western press itself. These comments are utilized by the Soviet press to accentuate the general Soviet propositions: that the United States and its allies endanger peace and prepare for war at the instigation of business and military leaders; that corruption, injustice, economic exploitation, and rank materialism prevail in the West.

The Sunday editions differ quantitatively and qualitatively from the weekday issues. They usually carry longer feature articles. *Izvestia* recently introduced a Sunday supplement *Nedelia* (The Week), which has twenty-four pages covering topics of international politics, national events, cultural and artistic affairs and has even carried English lessons in serial form. In format it is half the size of *Izvestia* so that it fits into the folded paper. However, it is sold separately for ten kopeks. *Nedelia* is an illustrated review and lists the entire week as the date of publication.

В БОРЬБЕ МУЖАЕТ ЮНОСТЬ ПЛАНЕТЫ

Пролетарии всех стран, соединяйтесь!

Коммунистическая партия Советского Союза

ПРАВДА

Орган Центрального Комитета
Коммунистической партии Советского Союза

Газета основана
5 мая 1912 года
В. И. ЛЕНИНЫМ

№ 261 (16847) | Четверг, 17 сентября 1964 года | Цена 2 коп.

Вчера в Москве торжественно открылся Всемирный форум молодежи. Посланцы пяти континентов из 121 страны мира, тысячи гостей форума, сотни представителей советской общественности заполнили Кремлевский Дворец съездов. Девиз форума — единство и сплоченность, солидарность молодежи и студентов в борьбе против империализма, за национальную независимость и освобождение, за мир.

В обстановке исключительного подъема собравшиеся восторженно встретили послание форуму главы Советского правительства товарища Н. С. Хрущева.

Торжественное заседание форума вылилось в волнующую демонстрацию солидарности прогрессивной молодежи нашей планеты.

ВСЕМИРНЫЙ ФОРУМ ОТКРЫТ

Открытие Всемирного форума молодежи в Кремлевском Дворце съездов. На снимке: в правительственной ложе товарищи А. И. Микоян, Д. С. Полянский, М. А. Суслов, Н. С. Хрущев, Л. Н. Ефремов, В. И. Поляков, Б. Н. Пономарев, А. П. Рудаков, В. Н. Титов, А. Н. Шелепин. Фото Т. Мельника.

С НАМИ МОЛОДЕЖЬ ВСЕЙ ЗЕМЛИ

Выступление
Альдо АЛЬВАРЕСА

Участникам Всемирного форума солидарности молодежи и студентов
в борьбе за национальную независимость и освобождение, за мир

Уважаемые друзья! Товарищи!

Передаю вам, представителям демократической, прогрессивной молодежи всей земли, собравшимся в Москве на Всемирный форум, горячий привет от правительства Советского Союза, от всего советского народа.

[...основной текст послания...]

Н. ХРУЩЕВ.

16 сентября 1964 года.

ПЕРЕГОВОРЫ Н. С. ХРУЩЕВА
С ПРЕМЬЕР-МИНИСТРОМ ОАР АЛИ САБРИ

16 сентября в Кремле Председатель Совета Министров СССР Н. С. Хрущев имел встречу с находящимся в Советском Союзе с официальным визитом Премьер-Министром Объединенной Арабской Республики господином Али Сабри, который передал дружеское братское послание Президента Гамаля Абдель Насера.

(ТАСС).

БОЛЬШАЯ ПОБЕДА СЕЛЬСКИХ ТРУЖЕНИКОВ

ВОРОНЕЖСКОМУ СЕЛЬСКОМУ ОБКОМУ КПСС И ОБЛИСПОЛКОМУ

Колхозникам и колхозницам, рабочим и работницам совхозов, специалистам сельского хозяйства, всем трудящимся Воронежской области

Центральный Комитет КПСС и Совет Министров СССР с удовлетворением отмечают, что труженики сельского хозяйства Воронежской области одержали большую победу.

ЦЕНТРАЛЬНЫЙ СОВЕТ МИНИСТРОВ
КОМИТЕТ КПСС СССР

Москва, Кремлевский Дворец съездов. Волнующий момент Всемирного форума молодежи и студентов. Делегаты и гости с огромным энтузиазмом встречают послание главы Советского правительства Никиты Сергеевича Хрущева.

Фото Е. Халдея и В. Бородина.

Soviet definitions of different reportorial forms underline the essentially interpretive rather than informative nature of Soviet news presentation.

Zametka. The *zametka* is a brief, one-paragraph news report offering some ten to twenty lines of basic information. It is:

> One of the forms of information, the basic form of newspaper material which reports the meaningful facts of the developments of general and political-educational interest.
>
> An active form of agitation with facts, popularization of successes, of achievements in all areas of life, and also a means for criticizing deficiencies or faults.
>
> One of the widespread forms in newspapers, it serves to illustrate the more important facts of Soviet activity and also of international life.[31]

Reportazh. *Reportazh* is the correspondent's detailed report with background analysis. "*Reportazh* is political agitation material. Like the other forms of newspaper information in our press, it agitates, above all with facts. But to agitate with facts means to give them a sharp, bright, convincing political tone."[32]

Otchet. This is a report or account of such events as gatherings and meetings and is usually accompanied by pictures.

The interview and reports of correspondents have technically the same meaning as their Western counterparts, with the addition that the necessary slant of the story is derived from Party directives.

Stat'ia. The *stat'ia* is a larger article that is distinguished from other newspaper forms by "its breadth of generalization and its depth of analysis of facts."[33] It is usually 80-120 lines long and most often reports new developments, technological or ideological.

Obzor pechati is a review or survey of the press.

Retsenziia. A review or critique of movies, plays, and books.

Ocherk. A short essay on contemporary events.

Saticheskie Zhanry. Here the tasks are twofold:

The main task of Soviet satire as expressed in the directive of the Central Committee is the struggle with the surviving remnants of capitalist consciousness in the minds of the people. That means the fight against parasites and bureaucrats, bribetakers and drunkards, against men who ignore and hide from their civic duties.

The second responsible task of Soviet satire is the unmasking of the bourgeois world, of the representatives of reactionary ideology, warmongers, the enemies of peace and democracy, and slanderers working to bring disrepute to the Soviet Union and the countries of peoples' democracies who work to strengthen the peaceful coexistence of peoples and the development of good relations among them.[34]

The *fel'eton* is a literary article with elements of satire and humor and a lively and picturesque style whose content is inspired by a "spirit of *partiinost.*"

> It skillfully uses irony and mockery for marked and express comparison. The good *fel'etonist* sharply and angrily exposes the remnants of capitalism in the consciousness of the Soviet people, omissions and shortcomings, all improper and decadent customs. The Soviet *fel'etonists* direct their pen also against imperialist reaction, against warmongers and their servants, against those people who fall under the influence of bourgeois customs and bow before "western" culture with all its deformity and perversion.[35]

The editorial (*peredovaia*) and the cartoon (*karikatura*), which together constitute the pure opinion reporting of the newspaper, are also clearly defined. Caricature

> is one of the most important forms of sociopolitical satire, ridiculing and exposing actual negative happenings taken from the life of the people. Caricature serves as the sharp weapon of political agitation. . . . Contemporary progressive caricature, the Soviet caricature before all others, participates in the struggle for peace, for democracy and socialism, mercilessly exposing imperialist warmongers and their collaborators.[36]

The editorial, "according to the letter of the

РОДИНЕ, НАРОДУ, ПАРТИИ—СЛАВА!

ДА ЗДРАВСТВУЕТ ВЕЛИКИЙ ОКТЯБРЬ, ОТКРЫВШИЙ НОВУЮ ЭРУ В ИСТОРИИ ЧЕЛОВЕЧЕСТВА—ЭРУ КРУШЕНИЯ КАПИТАЛИЗМА И УТВЕРЖДЕНИЯ КОММУНИЗМА!

ИЗВЕСТИЯ

СОВЕТОВ ДЕПУТАТОВ ТРУДЯЩИХСЯ СССР

№ 266 (14429)
Год издания 47-й

Пятница, 8 ноября 1963 г.

Цена 2 коп.

МОСКВА, 7 НОЯБРЯ 1963 ГОДА. Руководители Коммунистической партии и Советского правительства на трибуне Мавзолея Владимира Ильича Ленина.

КАК ЖИВОЙ С ЖИВЫМИ ГОВОРЯ...

ГОЛОС ЛЕНИНА НА КРАСНОЙ ПЛОЩАДИ

Скрылись на спуске к Москва-реке последние воинские части, участвовавшие в октябрьском параде. На мгновение замолкла Красная площадь. И тогда над ее просторами зазвучал голос великого Ленина, записанный в конце марта 1919 года на граммпластинку. Под ленинское слово, слово о Советской власти — власти народа, торжественно двинулись на площадь праздничные колонны строителей коммунизма.

Что такое Советская власть? В чем заключается сущность этой новой власти, которой не хотят или не могут понять еще в большинстве стран? Сущность ее, привлекающая к себе рабочих каждой страны все больше и больше, состоит в том, что прежде государством управляли богатые или капиталисты, а теперь в первый раз управляют государством, притом в массовом числе, как раз те классы, которых капитализм угнетал. Даже в самой демократической, в самой свободной республике, пока остается господство капитала, пока земля остается в частной собственности, государством всегда управляет небольшое меньшинство, в которое входят главным образом капиталисты или полукапиталисты...

Первый раз в мире власть государства построена у нас в России таким образом, что только рабочие, только трудящиеся крестьяне, исключая эксплуататоров, составляют массовые организации — Советы, и этим Советам передается вся государственная власть. Вот почему, как ни клевещут на Россию представители буржуазии во всех странах, а везде в мире слово «Совет» стало не только понятным, стало популярным, стало любимым для рабочих, для всех трудящихся. И вот почему Советская власть, какова бы ни была преследования сторонников коммунизма в разных странах, Советская власть неминуемо, неизбежно в недалеком будущем победит во всем мире.

Ликует, радуется, звенит песнями Красная площадь — трудовая Москва рапортует о своих успехах, рассказывает о планах на будущее, славит Великий Октябрь!

ОКТЯБРЬСКИЙ МАРШ СТРОИТЕЛЕЙ КОММУНИЗМА

ВОЕННЫЙ ПАРАД И ДЕМОНСТРАЦИЯ ТРУДЯЩИХСЯ МОСКВЫ

УТРО НАШЕЙ РОДИНЫ... Поистине необъятна, как движение времени, как сама жизнь. Рождается новое утро на Тихом океане. Плывут сияния на советских кораблях. С приходом солнца проснулся Владивосток, город машиностроителей, рыбаков, моряков. Его встречают труженики новых времен, новой эры в истории человечества.

Идет солнце с востока над нашей землей, идет над сибирской тундрой, посылая приветный луч землепроходцам — геологам... Встает солнце над алтарной Ангарой, покорной воле человека... Его встречают разведчики, определяющие площадку для сооружения еще одной мощной гидроэлектростанции — Саянской. Поднимется оно над Шушенским, где в конце прошлого века избы чумазый ленинского именно одной избы онкою ленинской избы учащейся эры и в истории наших зари освещало лучами нынешний день.

...

РЕЧЬ МАРШАЛА СОВЕТСКОГО СОЮЗА Р. Я. МАЛИНОВСКОГО

Товарищи солдаты и матросы, сержанты и старшины!

Товарищи офицеры, генералы и адмиралы!

Трудящиеся Советского Союза!

Нам уважаемые зарубежные гости!

От имени и по поручению Центрального Комитета Коммунистической партии Советского Союза, Советского правительства приветствую и поздравляю вас с сорок шестой годовщиной Великой Октябрьской социалистической революции.

С чувством большой радости и гордости за любимую Родину мы встречаем сегодня советские праздник — годовщину Великого Октября...

МЫ ВИДЕЛИ ПРАЗДНИК

Во время торжеств на Красной площади корреспонденты ТАСС А. Медведев, В. Степанов и А. Сурин обратились по просьбе редакции газеты «Известия» к зарубежным гостям, прибывшим в СССР на празднества, с просьбой поделиться впечатлениями о военном параде и демонстрации трудящихся Москвы. Вот что они ответили:

ДЖЕЙМС РОБЕРТСОН,
вице-президент национального профсоюза докеров и складских рабочих Западного побережья США

— Ничего подобного до сих пор мне видеть не приходилось. Глядя на ликующих демонстрантов, мы поняли, в чем заключается ваше «секретное оружие». Оно в единодушии и сплоченности.

ДЖОН КАКОНГЕ,
генеральный секретарь Народного конгресса Уганды

— Прежде всего я хотел бы отметить интернациональный дух праздничной демонстрации москвичей...

УИЛЬЯМ РЭТБОУН,
руководитель делегации национального профсоюза железнодорожников Англии

ДЖОН ЧАРМИНАН,
заведующий международным отделом Всеиндийского конгресса профсоюзов

СОМА БАЛАК ГИРИ,
член исполкома Всеиндийского объединения «Хинд мазду Субха», президент профсоюза рабочих сахарной промышленности

(Окончание на 2-й стр.).

Central Committee of the Party of 1922, is required to provide leadership, direction, to project the basic line of policy." The editorial, according to that instruction (which was given much earlier but was still treated as the basic guideline in a book published in 1961), "is not just discussion, not a debate, but a political instruction, a directive."[37]

It is abundantly clear from this discussion of the Soviet concepts of the role of information, the organization and control of the press, and the purpose underlying the selection of information that the Soviet press differs essentially from that of Western style democracies. The press is but one of the tools of the Party in the process of persuasion, organization, and guidance of the masses.

This conclusion is reinforced by statements of David Zaslavsky and Leonid F. Il'ichev. Zaslavsky discussed, in *Pravda* on November 7, 1959, the position to be taken by the press in regard to the West in periods of relaxation of international tension and thaw in the Cold War: "The warmer the international relations, the more acute the ideological battle."[38] Il'ichev, then head of the Agitation and Propaganda Department of the Central Committee of the CPSU, seconded that view and observed that the Soviet regime must continue to "resist the ideological offensive of imperialism, whose servants are doing all they can to revive the survivals of capitalism in the minds of the Soviet people."[39] The ideological battle is far from over.

CHAPTER THREE

CARTOONS IN THE SOVIET PRESS

The meaning of the caricature in our press is very great. It aids in carrying on the struggle with the remnants of capitalism in the consciousness and customs of the Soviet peoples, with all the stagnancy, backwardness and dying customs. The goal of caricature is the struggle for peace, democracy, and socialism, and the uncovering of imperialist warmongers and their helpers.

N. G. BOGDANOV[1]

Since the revolution the caricature has been "an inseparable component of Bolshevik newspapers, one of the elements giving face to the newspaper."[2] Gorky has said of the caricature that it has a tremendous political and educational character.[3] The cartoon at an early date assumed its important role in the Soviet press.

Caricature received wide circulation in our newspapers, journals, and in visual agitation as early as the years of the civil war. Its basic characteristics were determined at that time: sharp political purposefulness, ideological motivation, truthfulness, and accessibility. From that time the caricature was made an arm of our press.[4]

In style, Soviet cartoons fall into two distinct types. They are *druzheskii sharzh,* or friendly cartoon, and the *karikatura.* The first is usually devoted to Soviet leaders, artists and writers, or archtypes of Soviet citizens. It has been exceptional but not unknown for Soviet leaders in good standing to appear in cartoons. Deni, for example, depicted Lenin in *Pravda* of February 26, 1922; D. Mur, in *Krokodil* in the same year; and, K. Eliseev, in *Krasnyi Perec* in 1925. Khrushchev made his first appearance in newspaper cartoons in January, 1960. The second category is reserved for foreign leaders and customs and, to a lesser extent, remnants of bourgeois morality, domestic bureaucrats and administrative distortions. It is the *karikatura,* which is reserved for negative comment, that is the instrument of biting attack. The contemporary cartoon in *Pravda* and *Izvestia* is primarily the negative weapon used for assailing the West.[5]

Political caricature on international themes, as a rule, lashes those who are disturbing the peaceful coexistence among peoples. Our foreign political caricatures never set as their goal to ridicule this or that government system, to make fun of this or that nation. They uncover concrete instigators of international tension, organizers of the "cold war," bourgeois politicians.[6]

While in domestic cartoons the themes over the years were the kulak, the priest, the land-owner, the capitalist, and the bureaucrat (See Cartoons III—1 and 2, p. 16), in international events the newspaper caricature portrayed interventionists, monopoly capitalists, and during World War II almost exclusively fascists. After the war the cartoons returned to an old acquaintance, Winston Churchill, the symbol of the past glory of England, who gave way to the leaders of the United States the modern imperialist power—and to renascent fascist forces.

Like the editorial, news story, or photograph, the Soviet cartoon is an integral part of the party-directed press. Its message conforms to the information and opinion reported in the pages of the Soviet press. That *Pravda* sets the tone for the cartoonists of other Soviet journals and magazines was affirmed in the statement of Boris Efimov, a prominent Soviet caricaturist. "From the high rostrum of *Pravda* the political caricature began to speak very loudly and with unprecedented internal

and international resonance. On the pages of this newspaper a cluster of caricaturists were creatively reared, grew, and took their places in the craft of satire."[7] The editor of *Pravda,* under Khrushchev, Pavel A. Satiukov, emphasized the goals of the cartoonist: competence, precision, and great

ВОЛОКИТНЫЙ СТАН

На некоторых предприятиях, в министерствах и ведомствах плохо работают отделы рабочего изобретательства. Хозяйственные руководители мирятся с фактами волокиты, медленным внедрением ценных предложений.

Поточная линия бюрократической «обработки» рационализаторских предложений.
Рис. В. Фомичева.

III—2   RED TAPE MACHINE
by V. Fomichev

"In some enterprises, ministries, and offices the departments for workers' inventions operate badly. Industrial directors are satisfied with instances of red tape, and with the slow introduction of valuable proposals."

"A conveyor belt for bureaucratic 'processing' of proposals by rationalizers."

PRAVDA, October 17, 1956, p. 3.

ПОСАЖЕНО — И С ПЛЕЧ ДОЛОЙ!

В гор. Орске ежегодно проводятся посадки на улицах и в городских скверах. И ежегодно тысячи саженцев гибнут без ухода и надзора.

(Из письма тов. В. К. Монстрова).

— Ну, очередные посадки закончены. Сторожи хорошенько: через год проверю.
Рисунок В. Фомичева.

III—1

IT'S PLANTED—AND OFF MY SHOULDERS!
by V. Fomichev

"Every year in the city of Orsk trees are planted along the streets and on city squares. And every year thousands of saplings perish for lack of care and supervision."
"Well, the customary planting is finished. The guards are good, and after a year I check things."
The top sign says "Square." Goathouse sign reads "Guard of the Plantings." Paper in man's hand reads "Report on Planting."

PRAVDA, October 3, 1956, p. 3

sensitivity to the Party's needs; *"partiinost'* and *printsipialnost'* must be stressed and must permeate all their creative work."[8] The artists were admonished that satire is "the sharpest weapon and, as N. S. Khrushchev pointed out, it must be used very carefully in order that it not backfire."[9] A glowing assessment of the caricatures of Kukryniksy highlighted the values sought in the cartoon:

Unrelenting sniper shots at different masters of military psychosis. The text of the drawings is perfectly clear: necessarily, as the Communist Party requires thereof, to strive for peace, disarmament, peaceful coexistence of all peoples. The caricaturists ridicule without mercy, expose militarists who occasionally under the hypocritical mask of "peace-lovers" kindle military aggressive passions.[10]

To achieve these purposes, the caricature must be a penetrating commentary on contemporary events. "Caricature is a sharp satirical weapon. The few strokes of the artist's hand are not a simple drawing but a burning political commentary."[11] Purposefulness is essential:

> Caricature presents sharp, vital themes that have deep meaning. If a caricature treats an event or happening that is old or without current political relevance, it loses meaning. An accidental or mild theme weakens the satirical power of the caricature, reduces it to the form of an amusing drawing.[12]

To ensure that there will be no misinterpretation, Soviet cartoons, especially those in *Pravda,* often give a whole paragraph of explanation. The topic was frequently taken from a statement by Khrushchev on a domestic or international issue, and his statement served as the theme for the cartoonist to illustrate. "In caricature, as a rule, a very important role is ascribed to the accompanying text, which increases its efficacy."[13] The authors of this statement are "Kukryniksy"—a pen name coined from the names of the three men who collectively are the chief cartoonists for *Pravda.*[14] It is not surprising that *Pravda* adheres more rigorously to this theory than does *Izvestia,* whose cartoonists Fomichev and Efimov sometimes dispense with the lengthy textual explanations.

Through symbols and allegories, combined with jest, truth or half-truth, and moral purpose, the cartoon carries a powerful, thought-provoking message. Its power to create an image was starkly illustrated by Soviet novelist Abram Terz. "She shuddered with disgust as a newspaper cartoon

came into her mind: Trotsky, or Tito, or some such mercenary killer, pictured as a long-tailed rat and surrounded by his hangers-on, sat enthroned upon a hill of human bones."[15]

Although differing from its Western counterpart in its unmistakably clear message, its reliance on negative criticism, and in the large number directed against external enemies, the Soviet cartoon and the Western cartoon nonetheless have a common historical origin in the caricature of Honoré Daumier. Considered the father of the modern political cartoon, Daumier was a severe critic of the existing social order, its injustices and inequities. (See Cartoon III-3, p. 18.)

The Western cartoon emerged as an instrument of political propaganda during the French and American revolutions, expressing a political and ideological message that helped to unify the revolutionary forces.[16] As the years passed, the Western cartoon was used also as a weapon to arouse the masses in support of their governments' policies. The political cartoon contributed actively to the political propaganda of the American Civil War. The "yellow journalism" of the Hearst and Pulitzer presses utilized the cartoon in instigating the Spanish-American War of 1898. In World War I, powerful propaganda endeavored to convince the American people that the United States should enter the war on the side of the Allies. Cartoons contributed to the intense anti-German campaign, arousing great emotion by portraying the Kaiser as responsible for the deaths of innocent women and children on the *Lusitania.* Barbara Tuchman, in *The Guns of August,* speaks of the role of the political cartoon in Europe:

> National hatred of Germany had not yet taken hold. Among the first and most memorable of *Punch's* cartoons on the war was one that appeared on August 12 labeled "No Thoroughfare!" Brave little Belgium is there, a small boy in wooden shoes barring the way to the trespasser, Germany, pictured as a fat old bandmaster with a string of sausages hanging out of his pocket. He is ludicrous, not evil. Otherwise, in the early days, the cartoonists' pet was the Crown Prince whom they delighted to draw as an exaggerated

fop with pinched waist, high tight collar, rakish cap, and an expression of fatuous vacuity. He did not last. The war becoming too serious, he was replaced by the best known German, the Supreme War Lord, whose name was signed to every order of the OHL so that he seemed the author of all German acts—the Kaiser.[17]

While the role of the Soviet cartoon is quite precisely described in official definitions, that of the Western cartoon is a matter of less rigid definition. Two extreme views on the place of the Western cartoon have been posed. According to one view, the effective political cartoonist:

Must succeed in reducing an often involved political situation to a scene familiar to all. . . . Besides providing the key to an understanding of a political situation, the familiar picture gives the reader the added satisfaction of seeing the big shots brought down to his humble level by the homely parallel the cartoonist draws. Lèse-majesté is the life blood of many a famous cartoon . . .

The editorial cartoonist's job is more than to record the passing event. The cartoonist is essentially a kibitzer at the historical game played by mankind. Like all kibitzers he should have no inhibitions. His humor and wit must have free reign to be telling. His eye for the bizarre, the ironical and the ridiculous must not be clouded by fears and restrictions. He is at his best when he holds nothing sacred, even himself.[18]

The other viewpoint almost rules the cartoon out of responsible journalism:

The political cartoon is a caricature—an exaggeration, or inaccuracy, which should have no place in responsible journalism. The cartoonist must tell his story in black and white, literally and figuratively. He cannot qualify without weakening impact, and impact is everything to a cartoonist. Yet we know that the complex issues of today can seldom be presented in terms of black and white. . . . If our press is concerned with producing light instead of heat, then the political cartoon doesn't deserve better—excepting the handful of virtuosos who can supply our desperate need for helpful interpretation.[19]

But nearly all Western theorists agree on the necessity of the independence of the artist. Mi-

III—3

THE EUROPEAN BALANCE OF POWER
by Honoré Daumier

CHARIVARI, December 3, 1866

chael Cummings, the cartoonist for the conservative London *Daily Express,* exemplifies this spirit of independence. His sharp pen has criticized and praised all aspects of British, American, West German, French, Soviet and other countries' domestic and foreign policies for many years. His foreword to a collection of his cartoons sums up this independence.

It is said of some cartoonists that their drawings are propelled by a blowing passion against this party, this "ism," or that party, that "ism"; that they are filled with a messianic desire to reform the world, educate mankind, or propagate some particular gospel of their own. Please do not think of me in the company of those. I do not draw to the accompaniment of oaths against Mr. Dulles or Mr. Molotov, the working class or hard-faced businessmen—my only oath is when I lose my rubber or smudge the ink.[20]

The contemporary Western cartoon is a critique of both the policies of other nations and of domestic and foreign policies of its own government. The Western cartoon at times resembles the sharpness and biting criticism of the Soviet cartoon. But it directs its barbs at Western policies and leaders themselves, whereas the Soviet cartoons reserve their criticism for foreign enemies and a few domestic bureaucrats. Where the Western cartoon is an expression of independent interpretation, the Soviet cartoon is but another weapon in the Kremlin's arsenal designed to preserve the Socialist state, to advance the cause of Marxism-Leninism, and to battle its enemies within and without. As an instrument of Soviet policy, the cartoon serves as a mirror of Soviet intent and hence is a valuable tool for understanding Soviet motives and expectations.

PART TWO

THE CARTOON IN USE —
THE WEST AS RUSSIANS SEE IT

. . . Propaganda is only one—today perhaps the most important—of the three horses that pull the Soviet troika along its tempestuous course. Its yoke-mates are the greater abundance of material incentives and the threat of repression—now less obvious than in Stalin's time.

. . . The lack of the open use of repression . . . and this relaxation of fear have to be compensated by a double dose of propaganda.

. . . For all media of propaganda almost all the news-plus-propaganda is uniform throughout the country. All national and international news and views are handled in identical wording in Moscow and Vladivostok, in Leningrad and Ashkhaband. A small part of the space or time available is assigned to local themes. Even for these, the basic line is laid down by the "central organs"—*Pravda* and Radio Moscow.

PHILIP E. MOSELY
("How the Kremlin Keeps Ivan In Line," *The New York Times Magazine*, Feb. 19, 1961).

CHAPTER FOUR

THE STALIN ERA,

1947-1953

Both overly simplistic and overly shrill, Soviet propaganda endeavors to fix in the people's minds the image of a decadent bourgeois world in which horrible monsters—capitalists, imperialists, colonialists, bankers, blood-thirsty soldiers and policemen—rule tyrannically over enslaved people. The graphic symbols of this childish propaganda are always the same: the big belly, the bestial face, the colonial helmet, the sword dripping blood, the aspergillium brandished as a club, represent the oppressors; and spindly legs of the undernourished, shackled hands and feet, fists outstretched and desperate mothers bearing sickly children, represent the exploited and oppressed. In contrast to this bourgeois inferno, Soviet life is pictured as the best of all worlds. Everything in it, if not perfect, is at least worthy of admiration and especially rich in future promise.

SACHA SIMON[1]

Under Stalin the Soviet press was an obedient and unimaginative instrument for notifying the population of the decisions of the Party. Cartoons were blunt and clumsy in their stereotyped portrayals. Their subservience to policy dictates was especially vivid in this phase—through the noisy starts of campaigns, the sudden halts, the unexpected silences.

THE MARSHALL PLAN AND THE
BEGINNINGS OF THE COLD WAR

Traces of the wartime alliance did not linger long. The Soviet press had already begun its attacks on the United States in 1946. Press coverage of the United States increased throughout that year and the bulk of it consisted of negative and unfavorable comment.[2] After the Soviet refusal to participate in the Marshall Plan in June, 1947, including its forcing Czechoslovakia to withdraw its premature acceptance and preventing Poland from accepting at all, the end of wartime cooperation among the Allies, as well as the ascendancy of Soviet political control over the satellite nations was clear. Zhdanov's September speech at the Cominform meeting dispelled any doubts.

Cartoons in *Pravda* and *Izvestia* in the period June–December, 1947, were relatively few in numbers, and relatively mild in tone, without the strong or consistent anti-Western or anti-American propaganda that was to characterize the late fifties or early sixties. *Pravda* had ten cartoons on for-

23

eign affairs and *Izvestia,* eight, in those seven months.*

Of the four *Pravda* cartoons of early summer, one in June and three in July, three made reference to the Marshall Plan and American aid to Europe. The other cartoon, of June 28, directed against the radar defenses and bases in Greenland, featured a frightened General Eisenhower. (See Cartoon IV-1, p. 25.) On the subject of American aid, "Before and After the Paris Meeting," July 19, first showed the West European nations as happy children overjoyed at the prospect of American aid and running after Senator Vandenberg, who held a sack full of dollars; but as the meeting closed, these children turned bitter. They learned that the U. S. Treasury would be closed until July, 1948. Another comment on the United States economic "aid" to Europe, on July 25, under the heading "How Some American Gentlemen See the Road Toward European Unity," featured United States economic "aid" to Europe: an American was driving a steam roller flattening the sovereignty of European nations, while France and England rode as Uncle Sam's twin lackeys on the rear bumper. "Uncle Sam's Help to Turkey" was similar in theme.

Izvestia, in an anti-Marshall Plan comment on July 22, featured an angry and contemptible Uncle Sam informing anxious Europeans that "You came too early. See you in a year's time." In *Izvestia* a long comment by Efimov on September 25 attacked the vicious Hearst and Wall Street warmongers for perpetrating lies and slander about Soviet war preparations.

The six major *Pravda* cartoons of the year appeared in the period October 1 through October 17, and were all the work of Kukryniksy. The series of cartoons not only denounced the Marshall Plan, but also scored the fall session of the United Nations General Assembly and presented the United States as pulling the strings of power

and policy of its Western puppet-allies. The initial cartoon, on October 1, pictured Uncle Sam, Great Britain, and "independent" Greece; on October 2, it showed the "Congregation of Marshall Plan Worshippers"; on October 7 was drawn the architectural structure of imperialism, with the Statue of Liberty on top supported by Bevin, Blum, and others. All these pointed to the United States as the oppressor and exploiter of its allies. The United States' attempts to gain control of the United Nations were satirized by Kukryniksy in the cartoons of October 13 and 17—the first showing "friendly" voting according to United States dictation, the second presenting General Marshall and John Foster Dulles sawing away the foundations of the United Nations. In the cartoon for October 16, the United States was depicted as the hypocritical fighter for "democratic rights," as the oppressor of the laboring proletariat.

Izvestia, in six cartoons appearing in October and early November, concentrated on United States activities alleged to heighten international tension and on its intrigues and manipulations in the United Nations. In cartoon of October 2, Uncle Sam held a huge peg while General Eisenhower drove it into a wall marked "Foundations of the United Nations." Both *Pravda* (June 28) and *Izvestia* (October 2) depicted General Eisenhower in an unfavorable light that year. Because of his wartime popularity as the leader of the Allied armies, perhaps it was necessary to tarnish his image among the Soviet population.

The cartoon for November 2, an example of the "black-white" type, contrasted the enlightened Soviet Union (symbolized by the hand of a strong Soviet worker) ringing a bell to direct the world's attention to the perfidy of American warmongers while the powerless and unseemly figure of the American Ambassador to the United Nations (Warren R. Austin) tried in vain to halt the ringing. The October Revolution received due notice in the cartoon for November 7. This time Efimov presented the Statue of Liberty, a favorite topic, with a bomb in one hand and a money-bag in the other, surrounded by the United States' allies in

---

*Throughout the text, wherever total numbers of cartoons are given, these refer *only* to cartoons dealing with foreign affairs. Soviet cartoons on domestic issues were not recorded.

Рис. Бор. Ефимова.

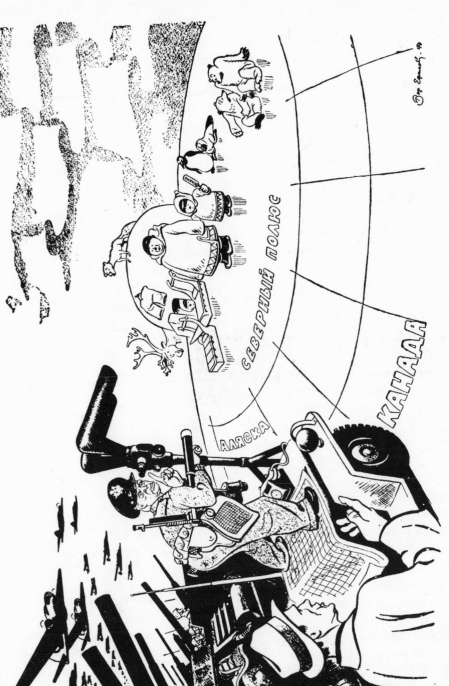

Рядовой американец. — В чем дело, генерал? К чему такая боевая активность в этом безлюдном районе?

Эйзенхауэр. — Как? Неужели вы не видите, какие силы противника сосредоточены здесь? Именно отсюда идет угроза американской свободе.

IV—1

EISENHOWER "DEFENDS HIMSELF"
by B. Efimov

"An ordinary American: 'What's the matter, General?' Why such military activity in such an uninhabited region?"
"Eisenhower: 'What?' Is it possible that you don't see an enormous enemy concentration of forces right here?"
Words on the globe: top, "North Pole"; to the left, "Alaska"; at the bottom, "Canada."
The little child holds the sign, "Eskimo."

PRAVDA, June 28, 1947, p. 4.

Europe. Winston Churchill lurked in the background.

In this concentrated series of cartoons in both papers in October and November, the theme was that of the United States as the leading imperialist nation—dominating and exploiting its allies, controlling the United Nations, conducting aggressive foreign policies, and impoverishing its own working class at home.

1948-1949 BERLIN BLOCKADE

There was restraint in cartoon coverage in 1948. This paralleled a general restraint in the press as a whole, the main feature of which was little news of a military nature and, in contrast to 1947, almost no attempt to indicate that America was preparing for armed action.[3] Throughout the year, anti-American and anti-Western cartoon propaganda was greatly reduced, and consisted of only four cartoons on foreign policy, two in each paper.

Both *Pravda* cartoons appeared in January (18 and 25). The first ascribed to the United States a policy of encouraging the "independent" European Socialists as a "third force"; the second assailed the guiding role of John Foster Dulles in West European rearmament, and accompanied an article on the same theme. The cartoon was employed frequently in Soviet papers to illustrate articles on important topics. Although there were no more cartoons, the campaign against the Marshall Plan continued through sporadic articles on the inside pages of *Pravda* and *Izvestia* in February and March of 1948.

Izvestia in the same year carried two cartoons. The first, on January 1, showed the Old Year greeting the New, with expressions of hope that the New Year would be better than the internationally tense 1947. The second cartoon appeared ten months later, on November 10, and contrasted the war-monger Churchill to Soviet peace-lovers. Churchill, who was no longer Prime Minister, presumably was accorded this special place in Soviet propaganda because of his famous "Iron Curtain"

speech in Fulton, Missouri, some two and a half years earlier, on March 15, 1946.

Although this was the year of the Berlin blockade and airlift (June, 1948–May, 1949), the Soviet press did not once mention through the medium of the cartoon the problem of Berlin or even the actions of the Western allies. The absence of almost all expressions or propaganda through the year, except on four occasions, was the most unusual feature of the year 1948.

The Soviet policy of maintaining total cartoon silence about the Berlin situation continued from June, 1948 through July of 1949 in *Pravda,* and through August of 1949 in *Izvestia.* Other topics, however, included American aid, and NATO.

Pravda carried six cartoons on foreign affairs in the period January–July, 1949, all by Kukryniksy. "Marshallization of Europe" pictured Uncle Sam carrying a Christmas tree with dollar-credit gifts that really meant huge profits for Uncle Sam. In late April two cartoons appeared. The first showed America's domination of its allies by picturing an American atop Bevin and Schuman (April 26). The following day, "Defense—American Fashion" featured a NATO submarine, with Uncle Sam at the helm, launching Churchill and Dulles torpedoes to intensify the Cold War. The May Day cartoon presented "The Club of Aggressors" (Churchill, Dulles, Spaak, Kennan, Blum, De Gasperi), and that of May 7, showed Harriman holding down Forrestal, who screamed about the imminent Russian attack on America. On May 26, after Forrestal's suicide, Harriman again appeared in a cartoon saying, "My friend, why did you leave me alone?" There were no cartoons in *Pravda* in June and July.

Izvestia carried only four cartoons between January and August. The first cartoon of the year appeared on May Day. It pictured the "North Atlantic Jungle," in which the allies hunt each other, with the United States a snake twisted into a dollar sign, and George Kennan, later to be United States Ambassador to the Soviet Union, was depicted as a mad dog. The dog seems to be a favorite representation for the Soviet Union's most disliked enemies. In the anti-Tito campaign, which reached almost hysterical heights in 1949, Tito was also frequently depicted as a mad dog. Kennan was presumably accorded this treatment because of his "Mr. X" article on containment (*Foreign Affairs,* July, 1947), which marked a turning point in United States foreign policy. As in the case of Churchill, the Russians had long memories. Efimov's cartoon of June 7, showed a strong and handsome Pushkin and his verses against those who denounce Russia. The cartoon of July 9, of the black-white type, portrayed the paper *Izvestia* as standing for democracy and socialism, and the Hearst chain press as representing the forces of war. Similar attacks on the Western press appeared regularly in almost every year of the Cold War.

CAMPAIGNS AGAINST THE UNITED STATES AND YUGOSLAVIA — THE SECOND HALF OF 1949 AND THE FIRST HALF OF 1950

Pravda, which had only six cartoons in the first half of 1949, presented fifty cartoons from August to the end of the year. This contrasted with a total of two cartoons presented in the entire year 1948. *Izvestia* likewise had two cartoons in 1948, and 56 in 1949. Two topics prevailed numerically in this period: American warmongering and anti-Tito attacks. The greatest number were devoted to Tito, twelve in *Pravda* and thirteen in *Izvestia.*

On June 28, 1948, the Prague meeting of the Communist Information Bureau (Cominform) denounced Marshall Tito and the other leaders of the Yugoslav Communist Party as deserters from Marxist-Leninist doctrine. However, despite the formal rupture, no cartoons appeared on this subject until August, 1949, more than a year later. Then *Pravda* used not only its own cartoonist, Kukryniksy, but also Efimov, who depicted Tito as the marionette of Washington or the "refugee from the camp of socialism and democracy to the camp of foreign capital and reaction" (August 13). Tito was always portrayed as a figure of small

stature in comparison to his imperialist bosses; frequently he was shown as a little dog, and several times the tail or even his whole body was twisted into the shape of a swastika. In one cartoon he held an axe marked "Fascist Terror" while he saluted Hitler, Himmler, and Mussolini (August 23). (See Cartoon VII-8, p. 122.) It might not have been unreasonable to depict Tito as the lackey of the West; however, his role throughout the war in fighting fascism and the German occupation is a matter of record. The Soviet cartoonists, technicians who followed the political decisions of the Cominform, exhibited distortion and inaccuracy in their portrayals.

As a lackey of the West, Tito was depicted as a frog, with the United States sitting astride him (November 3), or as a dog barking at the command of its masters, the United States and Churchill. Kukryniksy emphasized the betrayal of the socialist camp by showing Tito as Judas Iscariot. (See Cartoon IV-2, p. 28.) Efimov on September 18, reminded Tito of the fate of Laszlo Rajk, the Hungarian Minister of Foreign Affairs, who had recently been executed. Kukryniksy (September 20) portrayed Tito as a snake curled into a dollar sign and, on another occasion, as a parrot (September 30). Vasil'ev portrayed Tito as the mouthpiece of United States propaganda (see Cartoon IV-3, p. 29). Four different cartoonists were employed by *Pravda* to draw images of Tito. It is as if the cartoonists vied with one another in presenting him in the most despicable manner.

Izvestia likewise used a number of cartoonists to portray Tito in the worst possible light in its thirteen anti-Tito cartoons. In addition to the regular cartoonist, Efimov, several other cartoonists who were then relatively unknown in the Soviet Union joined in presenting Tito in various animal gùises: a cobra, with dollar eyes, who danced to the tune of Washington's flute (August 23); a frog in the midst of a swamp (see Cartoon IV-4, p. 30); a dog under the table eating the scraps thrown to him by Wall Street magnates (November 7). The association with fascism was also indicated—in Efimov's two cartoons in which Tito

Экспортно-импортный банк США предоставил Тито заё в необычайно короткий срок.

(Из газет).

КУКРЫНИКСЫ-49   Рис. Кукрыниксы.

Тридцать сребреников.

IV—2   THIRTY PIECES OF SILVER
                        by Kukryniksy

"The U.S. Export-Import Bank granted Tito a loan in an unusually short period of time."
Tito's cloak labels him "Judas."   *PRAVDA,* September 13, 1949, p. 4.

wields an axe imprinted with a swastika (September 11, 30). Efimov portrayed Tito also as a tottering Napoleon at the head of a collapsing Balkan empire (September 21); in other cartoons he was presented as a small insignificant character being misused by the West—as in Abramov's cartoon in which Tito was being skinned, as de Gaulle and

Churchill previously had been, by the United States (September 22). As in *Pravda,* to remind Tito of the dire fate that might befall him, Efimov noted the fate of Traicho Kostov, the Bulgarian Vice-Premier, who, like Rajk, was executed for his heresies. Nor were other Yugoslav leaders spared the barbs of Soviet cartoonists. Alexander Rankovic and Edvard Kardelj appeared, and Milovan Djilas was portrayed as the tool of American propaganda with a tongue in the shape of a swastika (November 24). The cartoon on November 7, celebrating the thirty-second anniversary of the October Revolution, showed a strong and powerful Soviet Union on the course that would defeat the imperialists and the Titoist traitors of socialism.

American warmongering accounted for the sec-

ond largest group of cartoons, with ten in *Pravda* and nine in *Izvestia*. Presentations in the latter months of 1949 stood in contrast to the absence of similar cartoons throughout the duration of the Berlin blockade, from its start in the second half of 1948 through the negotiations in the first months of 1949. As in previous years, the United States was shown in an evil and aggressive fashion, plotting to destroy the Soviet Union and the

Клика Тито — Ранковича, пробравшись к власти под маской друзей СССР, повела по указке англо-американских империалистов против Советского Союза клеветническую, провокационную кампанию, используя самые гнусные измышления, заимствованные из арсенала гитлеровцев.

(Из газет).

Рис. В. Васильева.

IV—3   TITO'S LITHOGRAPH
                             by V. Vasilev

"*The Tito-Rankovitch clique, which seized power under the guise of being friends of the USSR, by order of the Anglo-American imperialists has conducted against the Soviet Union, a provocative campaign of slander utilizing the vilest falsehoods borrowed from the Hitlerite arsenal.*"

   The printer is labeled "Tito," and the paper on the wall is marked with a dollar sign and word "Order." The papers on the floor are labeled "Falsification, Slander, Filth."

PRAVDA, December 8, 1949, p. 4.

Рис. Долгорукова.

В фашистском болоте

IV—4   IN THE FASCIST SWAMP
                           by Dolgorukov

The frog is labeled "Tito," who carries a piece of paper reading "Provocations,
Terror, Slander, Lie."

IZVESTIA, September 4, 1949, p. 4.

countries of the people's democracies. This image was not restricted to cartoons:

Moscow focused most of its postwar foreign affairs propaganda around the theme that American imperialism was plotting aggression. After a brief transition period necessary for cancelling wartime directives and allowing memories of the coalition line to fade, America was assigned in the Soviet horror spectacle the role vacated by Nazi Germany. The foreign bogey and the spirit of evil, both necessary for Soviet tactics, and both probably very real to the claustrophobic inhabitants of the Kremlin, were quickly found.[4]

The Marshall Plan reappeared in this cartoon barrage and was the subject of seven *Pravda* and five *Izvestia* cartoons. In most of them the United

States, profiting enormously from its own "charity," sought the economic enslavement of Western Europe. United States domination in Asia was the subject of two cartoons in *Pravda* and three in *Izvestia*. The United Nations warranted three cartoons apiece in the two papers, while NATO rated two in *Pravda* and one in *Izvestia*. As NATO was just in the process of organization in that year, it had not yet come under the full fire of Soviet cartoonists. The American domestic scene was the subject of two cartoons apiece in the two papers, while each paper carried one cartoon portraying the joint actions of the United States and Great Britain as the aggressive forces in the post-war world. However, greater emphasis was given to the theme of American domination of England—usually depicted by American trampling on the British lion or, at least, treading on its tail (*Pravda* and *Izvestia* each had three cartoons of this nature).

Anti-British cartoons were smaller in number (three in each paper) than those aimed against the United States; and the French warranted only one cartoon in each, while *Izvestia* carried six anti-Bonn cartoons and *Pravda* offered two. There were three generally anti-Western cartoons and one anti-colonial cartoon in *Izvestia*. *Pravda* had one positive cartoon—but more of a sketch—glorifying Lenin and Stalin as the founders of the Communist Party.

At this time the United States was depicted as directing West German policy, but in later years Soviet cartoons often reversed these roles. Another feature, in but a single example, was the cartoon glorifying Soviet achievements in science and technology and in the "struggle for peace." *Izvestia* hailed the Soviet explosion of an atomic bomb and Soviet success in breaking the atomic monopoly of the United States. (See Cartoon IV-5, below.)

The first half of 1950 continued this high pitch. In the entire year of 1950, *Pravda* carried thirty-three anti-American and anti-Western cartoons and

Рис. Бор. ЕФИМОВА.

Дули, дули, раздували,
Каждый день и каждый час,
Всем грозили, всех пугали...
В результате прочитали
Сообщенье как-то раз —

Сообщало миру ТАСС,
Просто, скромно, без апломба,
Что, мол, атомная бомба—
Есть у вас и есть. у нас!
Да-с!

С. МИХАЛКОВ.

IV—5

U.S. ATOMIC MONOPOLY!!!
TASS Communique of September 25
by B. Efimov

"They bragged, bragged, bragged,
Every day and every hour,
They threatened all, and frightened all . . .

As a result one day they read a communique,
From TASS to the world, reporting ..
Simply, humbly, without conceit
That, yes, we have the atom bomb
Just like you!
Yessir!"

—S. Mikhalkov

IZVESTIA, October 8, 1949, p. 4.

Среди кандидатов на получение в этом году так называемой Нобелевской «премии мира» числятся Черчилль, Трумэн, Маршалл и греческий король Павел.

(Из газет).

IV—6   PREPARATION FOR A NEW WAR!
by Kukryniksy

"Among the candidates for this year's so-called Nobel 'Peace Prize' are Churchill, Truman, Marshall, and Greek King Paul."

PRAVDA, March 4, 1950, p. 8.

Izvestia fifty-two. All but one of the *Pravda* cartoons appeared before June 21. *Izvestia* concentrated forty-six of its fifty-two cartoons in the period before May 14, that is, before the initiation of the Korean conflict. Of the total of eighty-five in both papers only seven cartoons appeared in the second half of the year after the start of the Korean War.

In 1950–1951, as in 1948–1949, the Soviet Union did not comment extensively through the cartoon on the serious conflict involved. Soviet anti-American and anti-Western propaganda (see

Cartoon IV–6, above), however, had been extensive *prior to* the beginning of the conflict, a fact that makes the contrast even more striking than in 1948; and, throughout the course of the year, anti-American comments outnumbered anti-Western, 32 to 10 in *Pravda,* 37 to 15 in *Izvestia.*

The New Year's Day cartoon had a large and very involved layout, with extensive labeling, many characters and subdivisions. The *Pravda* 1950 New Year's Day cartoon set the theme for the entire year: a composite portrayal of the aggressive, ugly West, its military leaders Eisenhower and Montgomery, American monopoly capital, imperialism, the Marshall Plan, and the Hitlerite vestiges associated with Western Germany. All of these topics were to be treated separately in other cartoons throughout the year.

American democracy and civil liberties were subjected to scrutiny and found wanting. Cartoons (two in *Pravda* and two in *Izvestia*) "revealed" that the United States solved its problem of agricultural surpluses by dumping food into the ocean while workers were left to starve; that the progressive American Communists were severely persecuted; and that the Statue of Liberty symbolized nothing so much as American hypocrisy. The cartoon which appeared in *Pravda* on March 23 (reprinted from *Komsomol'skaia Pravda*) treated the Statue of Liberty in the following manner: it stated that during the last four years, 830,000 Americans had been deported to their native lands because of pro-communist leanings and suggested that the Statue of Liberty itself should be returned to France. *Komsomol'skaia Pravda* generally featured topics in a more sensational manner, with less accuracy, to achieve a quick impact on its youthful readers.

United States imperialism in Europe (NATO and its economic aspect, the Marshall Plan) was attacked in three cartoons in *Pravda* and six in *Izvestia*. Boris Efimov, the dean of Soviet cartoonists, foreshadowed in *Izvestia* the new theme of the intimate relation between Hitler's imperialism and the American variety. He portrayed King Leopold of Belgium, who suffered first from Hitler's pressures, as being subject to the same treatment from the United States.

United States imperialism in England was the subject of four cartoons each in *Pravda* and *Izvestia*. In 1950, Great Britain alone of the European powers was in a strong position and thus warranted the separate and special attention of *Pravda* cartoonists. Churchill was often alluded to as the prime anti-Communist personality and was the target of the most bitter denunciations. Cartoons particularly emphasized the conflict of interests between the United States and Great Britain in the

economic sphere, as evidenced by the sterling-dollar rivalry.

General Douglas MacArthur usually symbolized United States imperialism in Asia and its aid to the Asian "reactionary" forces of Chiang Kai-shek and Japanese nationalists (*Pravda*, three cartoons, *Izvestia* five). The more general warmongering activities of the United States were assailed through the personalities of Eisenhower, Acheson, Bradley, or through such symbols as the munitions-maker monopoly.

Soviet charges of bacteriological warfare during the Korean War were foreshadowed by an Efimov cartoon in *Izvestia* on May 12, 1950. Entitled "Tokyo Marionette" (see Cartoon IV-7, p. 34), it depicted General MacArthur wielding a club and using Prime Minister Yoshida as a hand puppet. The Prime Minister is screaming "Ban the Communist Party." MacArthur's other hand contains handcuffs; rats and plans for bacteriological warfare are to be seen in his military bag. Perhaps the Moscow propaganda machine planned its propaganda far in advance of the commencement of Korean hostilities.

Comments on the British internal scene (one in *Pravda*, four in *Izvestia*) centered on the forthcoming elections in which Englishmen had to choose between Attlee and Churchill, both portrayed as undesirables dedicated to non-cooperation with the peace-loving camp. Marshal Tito, that well-known lackey of the Western powers, was unmasked in his attempt, on the instigation of American imperialism, to disrupt Sino-Soviet solidarity and in his effort to build an aggressive axis (Belgrade-Athens military alliance) to threaten peace in the Balkans. Cartoons adjudged Yugoslav elections rigged and lacking in freedom. Two of the four anti-Tito cartoons were reproduced from the Cominform journal, *For a Lasting Peace, for a People's Democracy*.

The visage of Hitler, superimposed on the image of the West, was drawn by cartoonists of both papers. Efimov and his associates skillfully moulded the traits of the Bonn Government, the United States, Hitler, and the Kaiser into a single aggressive force that threatened peace and the Soviet Union (*Pravda* had one, *Izvestia,* two cartoons on that theme).

Only one anti-colonial cartoon appeared—in *Pravda.* Another historical amalgam was achieved when *Pravda* combined de Gaulle and Hitler. *Izvestia* likewise attacked de Gaulle. *Izvestia,* which in the first six months of 1950 presented through cartoons a brief digest of important international happenings, also carried cartoons commenting unfavorably on the Italian-Turkish treaty, another Western aggressive alliance against the countries of the peace-loving camp. One cartoon lamented the lack of punishment for Finnish war criminals; another, starring Acheson and Franco, showed the United States support of fascist governments. The

Токийская марионетка

Правительство Иосида, по указанию Макартура, готовит запрещение японской компартии.   **(Из газет).**

Рис. Бор. Ефимова.

Иосида на посту...

IV—7   TOKYO MARIONETTE, OR
           YOSHIDA ON DUTY
           by B. Efimov

"The Government of Yoshida, on the orders of MacArthur, is preparing to ban the Japanese Communist Party."
   Yoshida shouts: "Ban the Communist Party!!!"
   MacArthur's bag carries the words: "Plans of bacteriological warfare."

IZVESTIA, May 12, 1950, p. 2.

United States Ambassador to Bulgaria was loudly accused in one cartoon of spying and plotting to overthrow that People's Democracy.

The "black-white" cartoons that juxtaposed within the same cartoon the image of the West, particularly the United States, and that of the Soviet Union and other progressive nations of the Communist bloc, constituted only a small portion of the total cartoon output. Boris Efimov depicted the dollar and the pound in a chronic state of crisis but the ruble as a strong and stable currency —to prove that instability is inherent in the capitalist world and strength equally inherent in the socialist camp. A second cartoon contrasted "free" Soviet elections to the farce of elections in the West. A third topic appearing in four cartoons each in *Pravda* and *Izvestia* concerned the signatures on "peace petitions" throughout the world, again with the Soviet Union as the progressive force and the Western World as the warmonger.

THE KOREAN WAR AND
STALIN'S DEATH, 1950-1953

The second half of 1949 and the first half of 1950 saw the largest number of cartoons in both papers (*Pravda* had 82 and *Izvestia,* 100) in the entire period 1947–1958. In the 18 months following the outbreak of hostilities in Korea until the end of 1951, only four cartoons appeared in *Pravda* and twelve in *Izvestia*. This abrupt and severe cutback in cartoon comment during the most crucial months of the Korean conflict was startling. It resembled the paucity of cartoon comment in both papers during the previous peak of tension during the Berlin blockade.

Pravda carried only one cartoon in 1950 after the Korean invasion in June. This cartoon appeared on September 21. In an especially gruesome way it depicted General MacArthur and the United Nations, the "aggressors" in Korea, laughing at dead Korean children.

Izvestia carried six cartoons between the outbreak of the conflict in Korea and December 1950.

The United Nations-United States "aggression" in Korea was mentioned in two of them, those of July 12 and August 12. The latter openly stated that the United States and South Korea had initiated the attack on North Korea. Two others (July 11, November 12) dealt with the subject of signatures on peace petitions and praised the Soviet Union; that of August 10, focused on Acheson as the chairman of American warmongering; and on August 29, Churchill, Adenauer, and the United States were shown constructing a European aggressive alliance.

Throughout the entire year of 1951 *Pravda* carried three cartoons. Only one cartoon, that of February 16, dealt with "American Interventionists on Korean Soil." It accused American gangsters of beheading Korean patriots. The two other *Pravda* cartoons depicted "General-Apostle Eisenhower" (see Cartoon IV-8, p. 36), as a warmonger, and Prime Minister Attlee as a peacemaker who accepted U. S. bombs behind his back. These cartoons appeared in January and February, 1951. *Pravda* readers were left without further cartoon comment until February, 1952.

In 1951 *Izvestia* had six cartoons. In the first, on April 1, Acheson carried a whip in the form of a dollar sign to direct the members of NATO, who performed according to his will. In the May Day cartoon, dedicated to peace, a worker swept away a spider web containing three spiders: Winston Churchill, Harry Truman, and Adolf Hitler. Following the summer silence, the September 13 cartoon featured Acheson as an auctioneer forcing the United Kingdom, France, and other nations to sign the peace treaty with Japan; Prime Minister Yoshida sat beside Acheson. On October 3, Adenauer appeared as a juggler sitting on the shoulders of the leader of the West German Social Democratic Party, Kurt Schumacher; his juggling balls formed a dollar sign, and John J. McCloy applauded from his theatre box. On November 7, another holiday, both Soviet and foreign workers carrying a banner "For Peace, For Democracy," confronted the tiny figures of Truman and Churchill. The last cartoon of 1951 appeared on

IV—8

DWIGHT EISENHOWER IN ROME
by Kukryniksy

The halo reads: "General-Apostle Eisenhower."
The briefcase is labeled "Military Plans."

PRAVDA, January 23, 1951, p. 4.

November 22, and again attacked Acheson and Wall Street for posing as defenders of peace.

With the coming of a stalemate in the Korean War, the commencement of armistice negotiations, and the decreasing probability of the conflict spreading from a local to a general war, the cartoon attack against the West resumed in 1952 and 1953 and bitterly assailed American and United Nations intervention in Korea.

Pravda carried 24 cartoons in 1952 and 29 in 1953; *Izvestia* 16 and 15. Cartoons were in two batches: January–June, 1952, and November 1952–March 1953.

The major villain of Soviet cartoons remained the United States. Nineteen out of 24 *Pravda*

cartoons attacked the United States in 1952, and 20 out of 29 did so in 1953. *Izvestia* had 14 out of 16 cartoons of anti-American content in 1952 and 11 out of 15 in 1953. The largest single group of 1952 *Pravda* cartoons, nine, was dedicated to the Korean conflict. Four cartoons accused the United States of carrying on bacteriological warfare through the United Nations, the State Department (see Cartoon IV-9, below), and American generals, all of whom were dumping rats and vermin onto Korean soil. *Izvestia* had two similar cartoons on bacteriological warfare in Korea in 1952, and one showing Adenauer preparing for bacteriological warfare on the orders of American authorities (December 13, 1952).

IV—9

THEIR WORDS AND DEEDS . . .
by Kukryniksy

"The American aggressors and their followers deny only that they are conducting bacteriological warfare. However, they don't even dare condemn germs as weapons. They don't even dare speak for their prohibition."

The letter says: "America is not conducting bacteriological warfare! — Acheson." He is standing in a rocket labeled "U.N."

PRAVDA, April 3, 1952, p. 4.

Five other *Pravda* cartoons on the topic of Korea accused the United States of "murder and money-making," of applying Hitlerite tactics, of using "brain-washing" and force to prevent North Korean prisoners of war from returning, and of using United Nations resolutions to cover up the aggressive plans in Korea. *Izvestia* also protested United States "prevention" of the repatriation of North Korean soldiers.

The United States domination of NATO was the major topic of five *Pravda* cartoons and of three in *Izvestia*. The Kukryniksy cartoon of June 2, 1952, showed French demonstrations against NATO Supreme Commander General Ridgway, calling him the "murderer" from Korea. Two other Kukryniksy cartoons noted United States domination of Great Britain, one showing the subordinate role of Lord Mountbatten in the Mediterranean

НЕ ОСТАНОВИТЕ!

IV—10

YOU WON'T STOP IT!
by B. Efimov

"How can you forbid and turn back
The peace movement which every day spreads further
    and further!
Powerless are the gentlemen, who wish to stand in
    the way
Of the struggle for the cause of peace in the world."
                                S. Mikhalkov

The locomotive carries a sign, "For Peace!" The posters say: "Halt!", "Stop!", "Back!", "Prohibit!", and "A New War Is Inevitable!"

IZVESTIA, May 1, 1952, p. 4.

GRECO-TURKO-TITO AXIS
by N. Dolgorukov

*"U.S. ruling circles are forcibly uniting the so-called
'Balkan sector' of the aggressive Atlantic Alliance by
putting Greece, Turkey and Titoist Yugoslavia into it."
The broken axis in the foreground is labeled
"Berlin-Rome-Tokyo."*

PRAVDA, January 5, 1953, p. 4.

and the other, the trampling of the helpless British lion by American bombers. *Izvestia's* cartoons on NATO were similar in theme to those of *Pravda* and condemned the West for war hysteria.

Another group of cartoons attacked West Germany. Although only four *Pravda* and two *Izvestia* cartoons dealt primarily with Western Germany as a continuation of Hitler's Germany, many other cartoons featured the Nazi-like Adenauer and other Germans as a major threat to peace. Germany, along with the United States, was depicted

as a dangerous and sinister power. (See Cartoon IV-10, p. 37.)

Other cartoons discussed United States domination of the United Nations and UNESCO, United States economic imperialism and exploitation of its Western allies, and the Western press which, along with the press of Yugoslavia, was pictured as serving the interests of Wall Street magnates. United States interference in the internal affairs of the French Government, and American training of Adenauer's West Germany to police Europe were further comments. A *Pravda* cartoon of December 13, 1952, called for the lifting of the American "iron curtain" that was preventing "peace lovers" from visiting the Vienna "Peace Congress." FBI suppression of freedom, or the judicial ban on the performance, in Pittsburgh, of a symphony by an American composer and dedicated to the Soviet Union, provided a sample of the domestic problems of the United States.

Prominent world personalities continued to appear in *Pravda* and *Izvestia* cartoons, including, in addition to those already noted, Clement Attlee, Dean Acheson, and Trygve Lie. Interestingly, although Churchill had appeared frequently in Soviet cartoons when he was not in office, he appeared only occasionally as Britain's Prime Minister, and not at all in 1953. Eisenhower, who became President in January, 1953, did not appear in any cartoons. On the contrary, a front page article reported in *Pravda* on April 25, 1953, Eisenhower's press conference about the United States position on the Cold War. The reticence to portray heads of state did not extend to Tito (see Cartoon IV-11, p. 38), a leader most distasteful to the Soviet Union, nor to Adeanuer.

In the last year of the Stalin era, 1953, both papers carried a rather large number of cartoons in January and February (*Pravda,* 14; *Izvestia,* 9). Cartoons ceased suddenly in March. Soviet cartoons did not record Stalin's death on March 6, 1953, nor the East Berlin uprising three months later. Except for an *Izvestia* cartoon in May, there were no cartoons in either paper from March 6 until the second half of October. This was the most significant aspect of cartoon behavior in 1953.

It was characteristic of the Stalin era that the subjects of cartoons were not relevant to contemporary events. They failed to mention domestic developments, including the Nineteenth Party Congress in October, 1952, which received no comment at all. The following international events likewise received no recognition: Communist China's entry into the Korean War; the Korean armistice negotiations; the Soviet Economic Conference for Underdeveloped Nations, in early 1952. The cartoons were pure propaganda of a rather clumsy type, with little bearing on events taking place. Subsequent years were to show some slight improvement in this respect.

CHAPTER FIVE

THE RISE OF KHRUSHCHEV,

1954-1960

Perhaps the greatest single source of distortion in foreign affairs derives from the image of "the enemy" which is deeply imbedded in Marxist-Leninist patterns of thought. The politics of Communism are built around the concept of the implacable capitalist adversary who has to be disarmed and defeated lest he in turn annihilate Communism.

MERLE FAINSOD[1]

POST-STALIN TRANSITION AND THE KOREAN TRUCE, 1953-1954

After a six-month silence following Stalin's death, *Pravda* resumed on October, 17, 1953, the same anti-Western and anti-American line it had pursued in the first two months of 1953. Even the number of cartoons that appeared in the last quarter of the year was about the same as in the first quarter: 14 v. 15.

The cartoon of October 17 depicted Franco's signing a military treaty with the United States, witnessed by Hitler's well-satisfied ghost. Two other October cartoons stressed divisions among the allies: the United States and Great Britain pushed France toward the West German Bundeswehr; Adenauer attempted to seduce the Gallic rooster.

November had the largest number of cartoons, seven. They condemned: United States refusal to admit the Red Chinese to the United Nations; the award of the Nobel Peace Prize to General Mar-

shall (see Cartoon V-1, p. 41); the United States choice of Adenauer as a pillar of Western defense; Adenauer, for seeking to join the Western defense system. They accused the United States of financially starving Great Britain and they attacked the United States for encouraging Chiang Kai-shek and Syngman Rhee to sign a friendship pact. The November 7, Kukryniksy cartoon was a typical "holiday" sketch and offered a review of events taking place in the "Atlantic Pact." (See Cartoon V-2, p. 42.) Most of the stereotyped symbolism of individual cartoons throughout the year could be found in this involved drawing.

December was a quieter month; only four cartoons appeared, all directed against the United States. They accused the United States of using the United Nations as a forum for slandering North Korea; for spending 100 million dollars for spying; for stimulating the aggressiveness of German militarists; and they condemned American and British monopolies for fighting over Iranian oil.

Following Stalin's death, *Izvestia* had six cartoons in 1953. On May 3, the forces of "peace" scattered the usual collection of warmongers: fascists, Chiang Kai-shek, Yoshida, etc. On November 9, *Izvestia* seconded the *Pravda* cartoon and showed enemies of the Soviet Union trying to find their way out of a maze. On December 3, another favorite *Pravda* theme showed the United States taking oil from Great Britain. American domestic terror, the Ku Klux Klan and disrespect for the Constitution of the United States appeared on December 5. October 30, and December 12, cartoons showed the instrumental roles of John Foster Dulles and General Speidel in preparing a retaliatory attack on the Soviet Union.

In 1954, *Pravda* cartoons were more evenly spread throughout the year and differed little in numbers or content from the years immediately preceding or following. It had twenty-four cartoons which resembled those already noted in the sharpness of their anti-American or anti-Western barbs. Although the style of the newspaper underwent a minor change after Stalin's death (there were no longer the space-consuming telegrams of praise to the leader), the cartoon varied not at all.

The major issue in 1954 was division within the West caused by West Germany's progressive reintegration into the European community of nations. In 1952 the European Defense Community Treaty to incorporate West Germany into a supranational defense system was negotiated. However, many interests opposed the treaty and, despite American urging, the French government failed to ratify the agreement. Fourteen cartoons depicted

Норвежский Нобелевский комитет присудил премию мира за 1953 год. бывшему министру обороны и бывшему государственному секретарю США, небезызвестному милитаристу генералу Джорджу Маршаллу. Это решение оказалось настолько несуразным, что даже американская реакционная «Чикаго трибюн» назвала его «скверной шуткой».

Рис КУКРЫНИКСЫ.

V-1

THE NOBEL PEACE PRIZE
by Kukryniksy

"The Norwegian Nobel Committee awarded the 1953 Peace Prize to the notorious militarist, General George Marshall, former Secretary of Defense and former Secretary of State of the U.S.A. This decision was so absurd that even the reactionary American Chicago Tribune called it a 'bad joke.' "

"To a militarist and businessman
The medal of fighter for peace was awarded—
They took the wolf for a sheep
But didn't unlearn him to eat meat!"
The ribbon on the sheephead hat reads "Nobel Peace Prize."

PRAVDA, November 4, 1953, p. 4.

В АТЛАНТИЧЕСКОМ ЛАГЕРЕ...

Рис. КУКРЫНИКСЫ.

Наглядные пособия по внешней политике Уолл-стрита

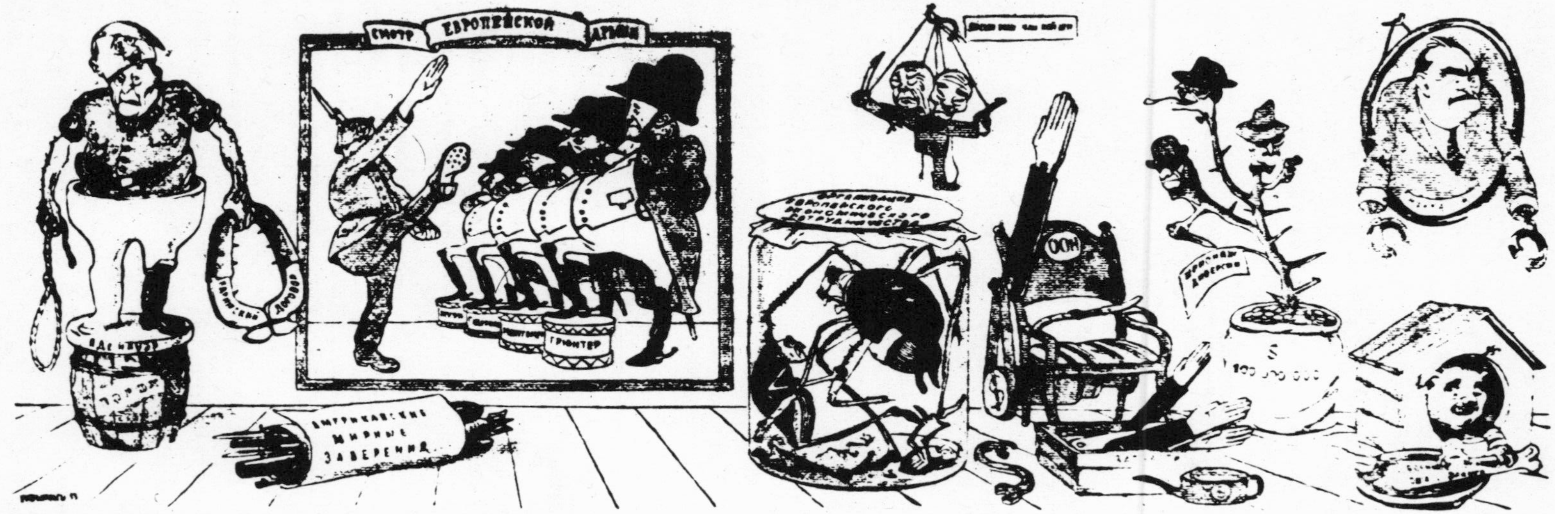

Слева вы видите небезызвестного Конрада III Аденауэра, претендующего подобно Конраду II (1024—1039) на вакантный пост германского императора, властителя Европы. Пока что Конрад III служит Уолл-стриту как кучер западноевропейского шестерика. В его левой руке хомут для немецкого народа, в правой — удавка, которой он грозится Франции, не желающей бежать пристяжной под кнутом немецкого кучера в американской запряжке.

На картине «Смотр европейской армии» вы видите четырех эрзац-наполеонов, производящих смотр гитлеровскому солдату. Это не так трудно сделать. Несравненно труднее выстроить в одну шеренгу народы.

Мы видим, далее, высокие образцы американо-европейской «дружбы». В банке (не международных ли расчетов?) — трогательные сцены из жизни тарантулов: в экстазе любви и верности мохнатый доллар оказывает бескорыстную, братскую помощь стерлингу, пытаясь освободить его от головы. Стерлинг в порыве чувства горячей благодарности отгрыз лапку у своего спасителя. На башмаке дне валяются ножки и рожки тех, кто уже до самого конца вкусил сладость долларовой помощи. О, дружба Уолл-стрита — это ты!

Над банкой подвешена главная опора империалистов США в Азии — марионетки Ли Сын Ман и Чан Кай-ши.

Попытка превратить всех сателлитов в марионеток, а Организацию Объединенных Наций в американский кукольный театр приводит к порче «машины голосования». На этот случай в ящике лежат запчасти.

На иудином древе, удобренном миллионами долларов, торчат фрукты, выращенные по законам рокфеллеро-моргановской генетики из белогвардейско-эмигрантского семени вида «шпионайчикова».

В будке дворца Эскуриал старый друг Гитлера и Муссолини — Франко с удовольствием обгладывает военное соглашение с США. Наконец-то он открыто принят в лучшем атлантическом обществе, где его до сих пор немножко стеснялись! Ему нехватает теперь только Нобелевской премии,

как [illegible] в живых [illegible] — Риос Тонито. Маршаллу премию дали [illegible]. Несправедливо! Не теряя надежд, он теперь [illegible] Вашингтон — Бонн. Но Франко мечтает и о более [illegible] бы переименовать Испанию во Франкоманию и на основе [illegible] присоединить к себе Францию. Тогда можно было бы назвать себя вторым Филиппом Вторым, зажечь костры [illegible] и назначить сенатора Маккарти великим инквизитором «Объединенной Европы».

Маккарти готов! Он радостно протягивает Европе свои руки-наручники, чтобы дружески зашелушить ее в [illegible] объятиях...

...Изучая наглядные пособия по внешней политике Уолл-стрита, народы Европы и всего мира получают совершенно точное представление о миролюбивой этой политики.

Д. ЗАСЛАВСКИЙ.

V-2

IN THE ATLANTIC CAMP

by Kukryniksy

"Visual Aids for Wall Street's Foreign Policy"

From left to right: "Adenauer" stands on a "powder keg" and holds the "Paris Agreement." The framed picture is a "Review of the European Army," while the pseudo-Napoleon generals are "Gruenther," "Montgomery," and others. Rifles, bayonets, rockets, and bombs are wrapped in paper labeled "American assurances of peace." In the jar entitled "Organization of European Economic Cooperation," the dollar is attacking the pound sterling. Above the jar hang Syngman Rhee and Chiang Kai-shek. The chair is labeled "U.N.," and the box below, "spare parts." The tag on the thorn tree says "espionage, intrigue." "McCarthy's" picture hangs above the dog house, which contains Franco grasping a bone entitled "U.S.-Franco Military Agreement." A text by D. Zaslavsky explains the pictures in detail.

PRAVDA, November 7, 1953, p. 4.

the United States favoring Spain, Germany, and Great Britain, over France. The British then proposed a revision of the Brussels Treaty so as to permit German entry directly into NATO. Final approval of this plan was reached in the Paris agreements of October 1954, and in May, 1955, Germany became a full member of NATO. The December 25, 1954, cartoon taken from *L'Humanité* depicted the United States, Great Britain, France, and Germany pressuring the other NATO countries to ratify the agreements. Germany was presented not only as dangerous to France, but also to England, and to all of Europe; suggestions were made of its superior strength. Its remilitarization, sponsored by Washington, was condemned.

The United States, the major villain of 1954, was criticized for its support of reactionary governments in Formosa, South Vietnam, and Korea. Secretary of State Dulles, symbol of the United States "position of force" policy, mourned the Indo-China settlement effected in this year. (See Cartoon V-3, p. 44.) There were no cartoons for two months at the time of the meeting of foreign ministers to settle the Indo-China question.

Other Americans were depicted that year. Senator Joseph McCarthy (who also appeared in November, 1953) dreamt how to turn the entire earth into a jail. Secretary of the Navy Forrestal was most bitterly attacked for his views on the Cold War; even Hitler's ghost expressed surprise to Forrestal at the war hysteria of American generals. On November 5, an anti-colonial cartoon, rare at this time but to become a staple feature in later years, called for "freedom from colonialism."

Izvestia in 1954, like *Pravda,* scattered its cartoons throughout the year. It carried fewer cartoons than *Pravda* (only 15), but a larger number of cartoons dealt with Asia. Yet it was the United States that was the major malefactor. Whether in the Turko-Pakistani alliance, NATO, the Paris treaties, Bonn's role in Europe, the rearmament of West Germany, or the anti-Communist coup in Guatemala, it was the United States that was "meddling" in the internal affairs of these countries.

There was little to distinguish between the two papers. Many cartoon topics were mentioned in both: lack of freedom in the United States; Indo-China; Germany as a threat to other European states. The only differences were the slight variations in technique used by different artists—the content was always the same.

1955 GENEVA SUMMIT CONFERENCE

The most interesting feature of 1955 was that neither of the leading Soviet papers mentioned via the cartoon one of the most significant periods of relative tranquility in the Cold War—the conference of the heads of state in Geneva, July 18–24, followed in November of the same year by a conference of foreign ministers to work out the details of the general agreements reached in Geneva. There were only 26 cartoons in *Pravda* and 15 in *Izvestia* throughout the entire year; all but three of the *Pravda* cartoons appeared between January and May, and the remaining three in December. From June to November there was a total absence of cartoon comment on international events. *Izvestia* followed a similar pattern, with 12 of its 15 cartoons appearing between January and May, one in early June, one in the second half of August, and the last one at the end of December. This official silence in cartoons was not echoed in the press reports or editorials,[2] which expressed an attitude favorable to the negotiations. It appears that when Soviet policy favored an easing of tension, even for a short period, the cartoon ceased to be used as a medium of propaganda against the United States and the West; rather, total silence was maintained. Soviet cartoon behavior ranged from anti-Western propaganda to temporary restraint from this; at no time in 1955 was a disposition favorable to the West expressed in the cartoon.

The main theme appearing in cartoons of 1955, especially prior to the meeting in Geneva, was the image of a Hitlerite Nazi West Germany. The specific objection was to West German remilitari-

Б.Ю. Ефимов

Новогодний стол накрыт.
Рядом ёлочка горит.
— Что-то гости к нам не едут!—
Аденауэр говорит.

Сам хочешь шкур от злости:
— В самом деле, где же гости?—

Нет гостей! А почему:
Да, должно быть, потому,
Что за этот стол садиться
Не угодно никому.
Сергей МИХАЛКОВ

V-3

"The New Year's table is set.
Alongside glows the Christmas tree.
'Why don't we have guests?'
Says Adenauer.
The host himself, grim with anger:
'Really, where are the guests?'
No guests? But why?
Well, it must be because
To sit at this table
Is pleasant for none!"

ATLANTIC HOSPITALITY
by B. Efimov

Signs from left to right: The duck is labeled "anti-Soviet game." Dulles carries the club entitled "dictatorial policy." He is surrounded by Syngman Rhee, Chiang Kai-shek, and Franco. Adenauer is "Bonn's Snow White." The cup of snakes is marked "espionage, terror, and intrigue." The box with ice is "cold war." Above the "new Wehrmacht" pig are the cannons labeled "armaments race." The boiling pot is "atomic psychosis," while the pressure cooker with a thermometer is "military hysteria." At the end of the table is the "cake of peaceful assurances." The Christmas tree of the "European Defense Community" holds bags of "American aid."

IZVESTIA, January 1, 1954, p. 4.

zation, as embodied in the Paris agreements which included West Germany in NATO and provided for its rearmament. France was portrayed as the helpless victim.

The *Pravda* New Year's Day cartoon featured "The New Order"—a gift to Western Europe from the uncle across the ocean signified European subservience to American militarism and economic imperialism. In *Izvestia,* the New Year's Day cartoon, "Around the World," repeated the outworn theme that warmongers infest the West alone, while peace-seekers reside in the East.

Pravda cartoons (seven) on West German aggressiveness, on the vestiges of Hitler, and on West German influence on Western policies were particularly bitter. The two cartoons of *Izvestia* censured more specifically German rearmament. Kukryniksy's *Pravda* cartoon on West German rearmament showed a reflection in water of the features of Hitler and his henchmen and of the atomic weapons given to West Germany. Other cartoons, with swatsikas and Hitler's caricature, showed the Paris treaties as but a weak paper padlock to restrain German militarism. The *Izvestia* cartoon showed preparations for the expectant mother, West Germany; the baby carriage was in the shape of an American tank, and the clothing and even the toys for the baby were militaristic in design. European munitions-makers sought their profits from defense contracts in the shape of sausages labeled with pounds sterling and swastikas.

While *Pravda* cartoons were concerned with the Paris agreements and resurgent German militarism, those of *Izvestia* concentrated on France's submission to American and German policy, its servility to American insistence on including West Germany in NATO, and on the probable consequences of German revanchism. *Pravda* carried two cartoons dealing with France; one noted its lack of government and the other its submission to German militarism. Others assailed the Paris treaties as such and American and British treachery against France.

Another group of seven in *Pravda* emphasized the "adventurist" aspects of American and British

foreign policy and military preparations. *Izvestia* had only two, focusing on the activities of both Britain and the United States in the Near East and on American policy toward China. *Pravda* cartoons stressed the dangers of placing atomic weapons in the hands of such adventurers as Field Marshal Montgomery or Admiral Radford, even though they were pictured as careless children playing dangerously with atomic bombs, rather than as sinister militarists.

The Western press received its usual lambasting in two Kukryniksy cartoons in *Pravda,* while *Izvestia* branded American disarmament plans as insufficient and the Western foreign ministers as evasive of the real issues.

In internal matters the only criticism of the American domestic situation, "Behind the American Iron Curtain," questioned whether Abraham Lincoln would have been fingerprinted!

Izvestia continued with cartoons of the black-white type: one in May described the Communist world as unified by its desire for peace, while the West achieved unity by entangling its allies in a ribbon of dollar signs. Another, "Balance Scale of History," contrasted the peaceful and defensive nature of the Warsaw Pact to the militaristic and aggressive Paris agreements.

In the period leading up to the Geneva conference, the most severe cartoons were those focusing on German rearmament and resurgent militarism. While there were several attacks on the United States and Great Britain, on the whole they were, by Soviet standards, quite mild.

Prior to the July summit meeting, cartoons in *Pravda* and *Izvestia* were numerous, but immediately preceding, during, and following that meeting and continuing through the subsequent meeting of foreign ministers in November, cartoon comment was extremely sparse.

The first cartoon after meeting, mildly critical, "Interview with an Ardent Worshipper of the Cold War," appeared on August 20, in *Izvestia.* It praised the decrease in Soviet armed strength by contrasting it to the fear and trembling of Western munitions-makers threatened by a decrease in the

некоторые буржуазные корреспонденты США и Англии распространяют клеветнические измышления о поездке советских руководителей в Индию и Бирму, пытаясь дезинформировать общественное мнение с целью оправдания политики колонизаторов и разжигания «холодной войны».
(Из газет).

Рис. КУКРЫНИКСЫ.

ВРИактивное оружие «холодной войны».

V-4

NUCLIAR WEAPON OF THE "COLD WAR"
by Kukryniksy

"Some U.S. and English bourgeois correspondents are disseminating slanderous fabrications about the journey of the Soviet leaders to India and Burma, trying to misinform public opinion for the purposes of justifying colonial policy and intensification of the 'cold war.'"

The wings of the paper and pen ducks are inscribed with the words "provocation," "lie," "slander," and "falsehood."

PRAVDA, December 9, 1955, p. 4.

price of shares of defense stocks.

The first *Pravda* comment following the July conference came only in December, when three cartoons appeared. That of December 9, "NucLIAR Weapons of the Cold War," assailed Western bourgeois correspondents and the press. (See Cartoon V-4, above.) The December 18, cartoon on Western aggressive alliances portrayed the Baghdad Pact as a wolf ready to swallow the small Middle Eastern nations that were its members.

The third *Pravda* cartoon, of December 15, and that of *Izvestia* of December 23, were volleys fired at American support of the defunct Chinese government on Formosa and at America's use of its puppet, Chiang Kai-shek, to strengthen its vote in the United Nations. In the *Pravda* cartoon, the United States was depicted symbolically by an arm, with dollar sign cuff links, holding a dust pan which bore the severed head of Chiang. Chiang's torn glove and ragged epaulet, hanging on a stick, cast its vote in the United Nations in favor of American proposals. This is one of the more distasteful of Soviet cartoons but a style by no means exceptional. An *Izvestia* cartoon used the profile of Secretary of State Dulles, on whose long nose sits Chiang waving a sabre at the mainland. (See Cartoon V-5, below.)

Рис. М. Абрамова.

«Представитель» и его покровитель.

V-5

"REPRESENTATIVE" AND HIS PROTECTOR
by M. Abramov

Chiang Kai-shek, sitting on Dulles' nose, waves a sabre and holds a sign reading: "We will not allow the entrance of the People's Republic of China into the U.N."

IZVESTIA, December 23, 1955, p. 4.

1956 SUEZ-HUNGARIAN CRISES

Following the 1955 Geneva talks both *Pravda* and *Izvestia* exercised restraint in cartoon criticism of the West and the United States. In the course of 1956 they presented only twenty and six cartoons respectively dealing with international relations. *Pravda* had seven anti-American, ten anti-Western, and six cartoons praising Russian achievements (the latter a relatively new development in *Pravda* and *Izvestia); Izvestia* had one anti-American, three anti-Western, and two pro-Russian cartoons.[3]

In October, 1956, the Hungarian Revolution—an event of vital concern to the Soviet Union—shook the Communist bloc. Despite its significance, cartoon comment virtually ignored these events. Only one cartoon appeared in *Pravda* on the subject of the Hungarian uprising. Even more peculiar was the treatment of Suez. A meager four cartoons treated this issue, three in *Pravda* and one in *Izvestia*. This certainly was a small number, considering the propitious opportunity for propaganda, and it was in marked contrast to Soviet use of the propaganda bait provided by the United States in 1960. One possible interpretation for reticence was Soviet embarrassment at suppression of the Hungarian revolt. Possibly the futility of hiding it completely from the Russian people made it expedient not to criticize the West for actions less deplorable than those of the Soviet Union.

The twenty-three cartoons in *Pravda* were fairly evenly distributed throughout the year, with a slight increase in November and December; three of *Izvestia* were scattered at the beginning of the year, with the remaining three in November and December.

The New Year's Day cartoon in *Pravda* was by Fomichev—"New Talent of Colonialists." In *Izvestia,* Abramov asked "Who Builds What?" His reply showed the West building a shaky war tower and Russia, the solid foundations of a house. The largest group of *Pravda* cartoons (five) before the outbreak of the Hungarian and Suez crises in October and November lauded the Soviet Union—

Планы хортистско-фашистских заговорщиков восстановить буржуаз-но-помещичьи порядки в Венгрии сорваны венгерскими трудящимися
(Из газет).

Рис. Кукрыниксы.

V-6   FIELD MARSHAL JOSEPH, COUNT ESTERHAZY, AND ADMIRAL HORTHY: "IT DIDN'T WORK."
by Kukryniksy

"The plans of the Fascist Horthyite conspirators to restore the bourgeois and estate system in Hungary were wrecked by the Hungarian toilers."
The picture is labeled "Hitler," while the paper in Esterhazy's pocket reads "List of My Lands."

PRAVDA, November 18, 1956, p. 5.

an application of positive rather than negative propaganda. One of these was a welcome address to peace-lovers, who were of course under the fraternal direction of the Soviet Union; two celebrated the Twentieth Congress of the CPSU; two others were devoted to May Day celebrations under the slogan "Peace and Friendship," with the Soviet Union and its Communist Party vanguard as the leading forces for the preservation of peace. The *Izvestia* May Day cartoon praised Soviet accomplishments.

In *Pravda* a cartoon critical of United States foreign policy appeared only once, upon the publication of the Yalta documents, which, it was said, would only aggravate ill feeling. One cartoon on American domestic conditions identified Senator Eastland as the successor to Senator McCarthy as chief suppressor of internal liberties. Banning of the Communist Party in West Germany demonstrated the general lack of real freedom in Western "democracies." Colonialism and Western bankers also were reproached, but without identification of any particular country. *Izvestia* carried in January a cartoon specifically against British warmongering, branding Air Marshal Slessor's visit to Germany as provocative. These cartoon comments aimed against the West and the United States were rather moderate, but the tone sharpened somewhat after the worsening of events in Hungary and in Suez.

The Hungarian Revolution and its suppression by the Soviet Army received no cartoon treatment in *Izvestia* and only one in *Pravda,* that on November 18 (see Cartoon V-6, p. 47), some time after the revolution had been suppressed. Symbols heartily despised by the Russian people were associated with the Hungarian revolution. Two other cartoons in *Pravda* indirectly mentioned the Hungarian events. One, on December 16, criticized the United States handling of the issue in the United Nations; another, on December 20, upbraided the Western press for exaggerating the revolution, saying that the press had manipulated the Hungarian tragedy for its own purposes.

Cartoons interpreting the Suez invasion were somewhat more numerous (five in *Pravda* and one in *Izvestia)* but still not extensive. The Western brand of peace-loving was illustrated on November 5, with preying Anglo-French-Israeli aggressors nailed to the "Pillar of Infamy," as peoples of the world demand "Hands Off Egypt!"

The *Izvestia* cartoon of November 3, and its only comment on Suez, also used the "Hands Off Egypt!" slogan. The last cartoon on the Suez invasion, in *Pravda* on November 24, skillfully tied American monopoly capital to the Suez crisis. (See Cartoon V-7, right.) Two later comments on the Suez crisis, on December 23 and 28, in *Pravda,*

emphasized again United States profits from the fiasco, while Britain and France lay defeated and humiliated.

Cartoons in *Pravda* in the first part of December depicted the Baghdad Pact as an instrument of the United States, while another cartoon touched on American manipulations of Europe, and a third attacked the United States "open skies" proposal as meaningless.

Izvestia seconded the anti-U.S. theme by presenting, on December 30, another positive-negative composite cartoon stigmatizing the United States attempt to undermine the People's Democracies. The United States efforts were frustrated, however, by the strong Soviet hand carrying a poster, "No Divisions."

V-7   Первые плоды агрессии...

THE FIRST FRUITS OF AGGRESSION
by B. Efimov

The inscription on the bag reads "Income for American Monopolies"; the words on the oil drum, "Oil for Europe."

PRAVDA, November 24, 1956, p. 3.

CONSOLIDATION OF
KHRUSHCHEV'S POWER, 1957

Although 1955 represented a thaw in the Cold War, and 1956 witnessed one of the most serious post-war crises, the number of cartoons in 1957, a relatively calm year, exceeded both of those years. In 1957 *Pravda* had double the number of cartoons (46) that it had in either of the two previous years, and 1957 was the highest year since 1949. *Izvestia* likewise had more cartoons in 1957 (17) than in the two previous years, but its increase was not so marked.

The last quarter of 1957, following Khrushchev's consolidation of control and the Soviet space successes, gave new confidence and half of the cartoons in both papers appeared in the last

quarter of the year. The intense cartoon campaign continued through January of 1958.

In this year the cartoon was used intensively in the propaganda war against the West in general, and the United States and West Germany in particular. The first half of 1957 saw cartoons against the "Eisenhower Doctrine": seven in *Pravda* and one in *Izvestia*. (See Cartoon V-8, below.) That doctrine was said to be not only detrimental to the Middle Eastern countries, but to British and French interests as well. While the doctrine associated with his name was attacked, the person of President Eisenhower was not.

Cartoons of both papers depicted the United States as the chief foe of peace, as a country that dictated policy to its allies. The latter pointed to America's attempts to prevent Britain from trading

V-8

AMERICAN BATTERING RAM
by Kukryniksy

The log is marked "Eisenhower Doctrine." Sign on the door reads "Near and Middle East."

PRAVDA, January 16, 1957, p. 4.

with Communist China. On January 27, 1957, *Pravda* carried the first of numerous cartoons protesting the appointment of former Wehrmacht general Hans Speidel as the German representative in NATO. (See Cartoon V-9, below.) June and July cartoons in both papers featured, among the other usual topics, a few cartoons urging that the United States stop atomic tests and halt the arms race. The French were again singled out as being tricked by the allies, this time by Americans who were giving arms to Tunisia, against the wishes of the French (*Pravda,* November 20). The *Izvestia* cartoon of December 29, warned France and Great Britain that the United States atomic bombers which flew daily over those two countries endangered their safety. A black-white cartoon in *Izvestia* pointed out that over Moscow there was a "peace flower" and over New York, an "atomic umbrella."

The traditional distaste of *Pravda* for Social Democrats was accented in a December 2 cartoon in which Kautsky was criticized for his statement that "Marxism is outmoded." A cartoon of December 5, ridiculed the term "people's capitalism" as a farce; and on November 24, a cartoon condemned the United States for using the fight against communism as an excuse to prepare for war.

The Western and American press and Radio Free Europe were attacked in one cartoon in each paper. Usual mention was made of United Nations subservience to United States foreign policy. *Pravda* had two cartoons in which the United States was condemned for raising the Hungarian question before the United Nations (July 8, and September 26); another depicted the United States dictating to the U.N. (September 10). NATO's annual December meeting provided another cartoon target. Danish and Norwegian refusal to accept U.S. rocket bases was greeted with relief.

The Soviet sputnik success in October naturally called for enthusiastic cartoon greetings. The first *Izvestia* cartoon, of October 6, praised the Soviet success, while the second one, of November 12, used Khrushchev's statement to challenge the United States Vanguard rocket to a space race. (See Cartoon V-10, p. 51.) *Pravda* also ridiculed the U.S. space failures in a cartoon of December 9, and acclaimed the Soviet satellite's one thousand orbits on December 11. On December 31 another cartoon greeted the series of Soviet sputniks.

Возвращение Ганса Шпейделя

V-9   THE RETURN OF HANS SPEIDEL
by Kukryniksy

Words on the hat read "NATO, European Army." Ribbons read "For War Against France," "For War Against England."

The story accompanying the cartoon provides additional information about his sinister role in the Wehrmacht and in the future development of NATO.

PRAVDA, January 27, 1957, p. 4.

In 1957 one could discern in cartoons the greater self-assurance of the Soviet Union. An open and sustained anti-Western, anti-American, and anti-German campaign was evident, a campaign that was to intensify in subsequent years, side by side with the "peaceful coexistence" drive of the new leader, Nikita Sergeievich Khrushchev.

1958 MIDDLE EAST AND BERLIN CRISES

This year showed a steady increase in the number of cartoons in both papers, almost doubling the number of cartoons in 1957: *Pravda* had 73 cartoons, and *Izvestia* 36.

The first half of 1958 was relatively calm, except for January, which had 17 *Pravda* cartoons, and seven *Izvestia* cartoons. Cartoons glorifying the Soviet Union and space successes emerged in strength. V. Fomichev's *Izvestia* cartoon of May 18, 1958, "The Three Knights," was a fine example of such a cartoon. (See Cartoon V-11, p. 52.)

The United States again was the major adversary and NATO, the Baghdad Pact, and SEATO were described as the centers of the Cold War intrigue. A continued effort to ban United States atomic bases overseas was coupled with another group of cartoons calling for disarmament. West German and Western armaments were condemned as having Hitler's blessings.

«Наши спутники вращаются вокруг Земли и ждут, когда появятся рядом с ними американские и другие спутники и составят содружество спутников. Такое содружество, такое соревнование будут куда лучше, чем соревнование в гонке вооружений, в производстве смертоносного оружия».

(Из доклада товарища Н. С. Хрущева на юбилейной сессии Верховного Совета СССР).

Рисунок художника Н. Фидлера

V-10

LET'S COMPETE
by N. Fidler

"Our sputniks circle the earth and wait for American and other sputniks to appear alongside and provide companionship. Such companionship and such competition will be far better than competition in the armament race or in production of deadly weapons."
—From the report of Comrade N. S. Khrushchev to the anniversary session of the USSR Supreme Soviet.

The Soviet sputniks hold flags entitled "Let's Compete!", while the earthbound U.S. space satellite has a drooping flag labeled "Vanguard."

IZVESTIA, November 12, 1957, p. 4.

Под Млечной дорогой крутою,
Созвездьем радостным горя,
Летят космической тропою
Три сказочных богатыря.

Блестят на солнце их кольчуги,
Что на Земле закалены,

И вихри метеорной вьюги
Могучим троице не страшны.

У них в руках антенны-пики:
Богатыри с недавних пор
В просторах необжито-диких
Несут научный свой дозор.

Оценивают веско, строго:
По межпланетной целине
С Земли каким путем-дорогой
В поход отправиться к Луне!

Владимир ЧУХРОВ

Рис. В. Фомичева.

V-11

THE THREE KNIGHTS
by V. Fomichev
Poem by Vladimir Chukhrov

"Under the Milky Way,
Bright like a joyous constellation,
Three fabulous knights
Fly along the cosmic trail.
Their cuirasses, tempered on earth,
Shine in the sun,
And the whirlwinds of a meteoric storm
Do not frighten the mighty trio.
In their hands are antenna spears:
The knights of recent times
Conduct their scientific survey
In wild uninhabited space.
They estimate solidly and strictly:
What route from the earth
Through interplanetary space
Is the course to reach the moon?"

IZVESTIA, May 18, 1958, p. 4.

Pravda devoted several cartoons to thirsty, money-worshipping capitalists and colonialists. In one such cartoon, Marx destroyed capitalism. Nor was the American domestic scene overlooked. A cartoon from the *Daily Worker* (New York) showed defense expenditures consuming all the money while the American worker went hungry; another illustrated unemployment in the United States; and *Izvestia* dealt with the racial question.

"Solidarity of the Socialist Countries," a rare application of the cartoon to problems of the Soviet bloc, pictured that solidarity as a massive wall that the drill labeled "revisionism" could not penetrate. Senate Majority Leader Lyndon Johnson appeared as a space monkey trying desperately to accelerate the American space program. (See Cartoon V-12, right.) Colonialism was mentioned in two *Pravda* cartoons in which Africa and Asia free themselves, and in one cartoon in which Latin America rejected the American satellite while wel-

Космические притязания сенатора Джонсона.
Рисунок И. М

V-12

COSMIC CLAIMS OF SENATOR JOHNSON
by I. Mandriki

PRAVDA, January 27, 1958, p. 4.

A May 24 cartoon censured United States aggression in Lebanon. *Izvestia* carried on June 15 and June 22 two cartoons accusing the West of sabotaging the prospects for a summit meeting. The summit meeting did not appear again in Soviet cartoons until after the downing of the U-2 plane. (See Cartoons V-13 & 14, this page.)

The Lebanese and Jordanian governments in the summer of 1958 requested that American and

V-13

PERFORMANCE OF A LENGTHY *DIPLOMATIC* "LULLABY" ACCOMPANIED BY THE *GENERAL* CHOIR
by V. Fomichev

The lyrics read: "Proposals for preliminary discussion about the question of a summit conference." "Western Diplomacy" is the label on the briefcase.

IZVESTIA, June 22, 1958, p. 4.

V-14

"THE COUPLERS"
by V. Fomichev

"Diplomacy of the Western countries is trying to hamper and delay a summit meeting by coupling together the most dissimilar problems."
The problems being linked by the West are: "Cessation of Nuclear Bomb Tests," "Cessation of Production of Nuclear Armament," "Reduction of Conventional Armament," and the "German Question." Man in the foreground carries a roadblock labeled "Dead End."

IZVESTIA, June 15, 1958, p. 4.

coming the Soviet sputnik. *Izvestia* derided former German rocket expert Wernher von Braun for the "poor" quality of American rockets. *Izvestia* also echoed *Pravda* cartoons and asserted the correctness of Marx's interpretation; that the United States is unpopular in Latin America; that French generals undermine the Fourth Republic; that the Baghdad Pact would fail; and that American bombers over England endanger British safety.

British troops land in their countries in order to preserve peace and order. This was the occasion for much more violent and numerous Soviet cartoon comments than those evoked by the Anglo-French-Israeli attack on Suez in 1956. Whereas there were in the latter instance three cartoons in *Pravda* and one in *Izvestia* in the two months of October and November, there were in a comparable two-month period during the Middle Eastern unrest, twenty in *Pravda* and three in *Izvestia*. Anti-American comment was much more prominent than anti-British and not only assailed the Middle East intervention itself, but also demonstrated the "necessary inner connection" between that event and aggressive American policies in the Far East. The Sixth Fleet in the Mediterranean and the Seventh Fleet in the Formosa straits constituted the "twin pincers of American imperialism." *Pravda* carried nine cartoons on United States imperialism in the Middle East, six on

Поправ Потсдамское и другие международные соглашения, западны державы потеряли право для сохранения своих оккупационных порядк в Берлине, как и в любой другой части Германии.

(Из газет).

«ВЫПОЛНЯЮТ» ПОТСДАМСКОЕ СОГЛАШЕНИЕ.

Рисунок М. Абрамова.

V-16   THEY "FULFILL"
THE POTSDAM AGREEMENT
by M. Abramov

"By modifying the Potsdam and other international agreements, the Western powers have lost the right to maintain their occupation troops in Berlin or in any other part of Germany."

The tree is labeled "Potsdam Agreement," and its top branch "Occupation Status of West Berlin." The saw wielded by the United States (dollar), Britain (pound), and France (franc) reads "Militarization of the German Federal Republic."

PRAVDA, November 30, 1958, p. 5.

РАКОВАЯ ОПУХОЛЬ...

Рис. В. Фомичева.

...требующая лечения

V-15   A CANCEROUS TUMOR . . .
NEEDING MEDICAL CARE
by V. Fomichev

The medicine bottle is labeled "Free City Status to West Berlin." The group of frightened people are the "Occupation Regime," heaped on "West Berlin."

IZVESTIA, November 29, 1958, p. 4.

British-American imperialism in Jordan, and one against joint Anglo-American aggression and involvement in the Middle East.

Aggressive American designs were the topic for four further cartoons in *Pravda* and three in *Izvestia* that extended the sphere of alleged American intentions beyond the Formosa straits and into Korea and Vietnam. On August 3, in *Pravda*, Kukryniksy depicted American warmongering by showing the United States lighting a war torch instead of the torch on the Statue of Liberty. One broader anti-Western cartoon against warmongering appeared in *Pravda*. United States disarmament evasion was asserted in one cartoon each in *Pravda* and *Izvestia* and United States economic imperialism in two cartoons in *Pravda*. In the August 25 cartoon by Abramov the United Nations, usually a symbol of United States imperialism and neo-colonialism, somewhat inconsistently urged Anglo-American forces to withdraw from Jordan and Lebanon.

The second Berlin crisis, that of 1958, was precipitated by a series of speeches by Premier Khrushchev in the fall of that year in which he insisted: that the Allies withdraw from Berlin; that the spy activities that constituted a "cancerous growth" be removed; and that unless this were done, a separate peace treaty would be signed by the Soviet Union with East Germany, unilaterally ending the four-power status of the city. (See Cartoons V-15 & 16, p. 54.) The six-month limit

Буржуи,
    дивитесь
        коммунистическому берегу —
на работе,
    в аэроплане,
        в вагоне
вашу
    быстроногую
        знаменитую Америку
мы
    и догоним
        и перегоним.

Рисунок Н. Долгорукова.   (В. МАЯКОВСКИЙ).

V-18

FOR COMMUNISM, FOR PEACE!
by N. Dolgorukov

"Bourgeoisie,
*   Marvel*
*   At our Communist shore—*
At work,
*   In the airplane,*
*   In the railway car*
We will
*   both overtake*
*   and surpass*
Your
*   lightfooted*
*   famous America."*
*   —V. Mayakovsky*

Sub-headline on the newspaper reads "Control Figures for the Development of USSR National Economy during 1959-1965." Banners around the derricks state the 1965 plan for production of iron, steel, rolled steel, chemicals and oil.

PRAVDA, November 18, 1958, p. 5.

Американское командование сообщило о создании в Италии ракетно-атомных баз США.   (Из газет).

ХОЛОДНЫЙ САПОЖНИК ГОРЯЧЕЙ ВОЙНЫ.

V-17

COLD SHOEMAKER OF THE HOT WAR
by Kukryniksy

"American headquarters has announced that U.S. bases for nuclear rockets are being built in Italy." Boot is marked "Italy."

PRAVDA, November 25, 1958, p. 5.

set in November, 1958, for signing the peace treaty was later extended indefinitely.

Although this new Soviet cold war maneuver did not arouse so much excitement in the Western as in the Soviet press, it was a source of concern to the West. The leading Soviet papers played up the issue extensively through cartoons and used this as a starting point for additional anti-Western and anti-American cartoons.

Treatment of the Berlin crisis marked a shift in propaganda policy. This can be seen from the number of cartoons. In the last six months of 1958, *Pravda* had forty-four, more than the total number for most years since 1947. The proportion of anti-American cartoons in *Pravda,* which sets the ideological tone on the West in the Soviet press, was greater than the first half of 1950, when cartoons were highly belligerent.

The Berlin situation proper, rather than more general anti-Western or anti-American commentary, was also the topic of many cartoons. Three cartoons each in *Pravda* and *Izvestia* dealt directly with the city of Berlin. Other cartoons commented upon such issues at NATO ("Transoceanic Training in NATO," "Cold Shoemaker of the Hot War," and "Changing Times") (see Cartoon V-17, p. 55), the increasing strength of the socialist

ЗЛОКЛЮЧЕНИЯ ФАКЕЛЬЩИКА ВОЙНЫ
Рисунок датского художника Херлуфа Бидструпа для «Правды».

V-19

EVIL FATE OF AN INCENDIARY OF WAR
by the Danish artist Herluf Bidstrup for *Pravda*

The fire hose under the Kremlin is twisted to read "USSR."

PRAVDA, November 7, 1958, p. 6.

ПОСТАВЛЕННЫЙ НА КАРТУ...

V-20

PLACED ON THE MENU
by Kukryniksy

The island is labeled "England."
PRAVDA, December 11, 1958, p. 5.

countries, (see Cartoons V-18 & 19) and growing West German militarism. "Detailed Approach" in *Izvestia* again struck at Western bad faith in disarmament negotiations.

The doom of colonialism was forecast with the aid of a proverb, "Who digs a hole for someone else, falls into it." In *Pravda,* using the positive-negative approach, a deformed and decrepit old colonialist strangled in the chains he had attached to Africans. Two other cartoons elaborated the topic of United States economic imperialism— "The Imperialist Trap" and "Placed on the Menu" in *Pravda.* The second drawing showed the American dollar sign as a snake trying to devour the British lion, which in this instance bore closer resemblance to a scared rabbit. (See Cartoon V-20, above.)

In this six-month period, the latter half of 1958, *Pravda* carried one cartoon on Soviet domestic problems and *Izvestia* 17—of which two were *druzheskie sharzhi,* or "friendly cartoons," and 15 critical of local shortcomings and bureaucratic bungling.

KHRUSHCHEV'S VISIT TO THE UNITED STATES AND THE "SPIRIT OF CAMP DAVID," 1959

This year of the Cold War commenced with Fidel Castro's January First victory in Cuba, was followed in March by the Tibetan revolt against Communist China, in the summer by Vice-President Nixon's visit to the Soviet Union (July 23–August 5) and the "kitchen debate," Soviet lunar shots, and finally, Khrushchev's visit to the United States, September 15–27.

The number of cartoons in both papers in 1959 exceeded all other years since 1947. *Izvestia,* with 138 cartoons, for the first time surpassed *Pravda* (113) in the number of cartoons, despite the fact that *Pravda* is published daily, and *Izvestia* has only 300 issues a year. This change was foreshadowed by the 1959 decree of the CC CPSU defining the tasks of *Izvestia.*

Pravda had 20 and *Izvestia* 24 cartoons praising Soviet space successes and the Twenty-First Congress of the CPSU. The *Pravda* cartoon of May 8, 1959, celebrated Sputnik III's five thousand orbits around the Earth, and *Izvestia* noted this fact on May 15.

After Khrushchev officially became Premier, on March 27, 1958, replacing Bulganin, he began to appear more frequently in the Soviet press and in pictures, and his statements were often used as the basis for cartoons. In the first six months of 1959, *Pravda* had four such cartoons, and they later became almost a standard feature of cartoons in both papers. All four of Khrushchev's statements dealt with Adenauer and the German threat to peace, and all included links to the United States as the major villain. The last cartoon depicted Adenauer

trying to scare Great Britain and France, while Uncle Sam calmly laughed (*Pravda,* June 20, 1959).

The largest number of cartoons in both papers appeared after May, 1959. An intensified cartoon campaign continued, with only brief lapses, into 1960, up to the Paris summit talks. The themes were still the same: "NATOleon BONNaparte" (*Pravda,* April 7); or the United States stuffing an Italian boot with atomic rockets (*Izvestia,* June 10).

The tenth anniversary of the North Atlantic Treaty drew the attention of many cartoons. The Pentagon was brought together with Nazi generals as the chief plotters in the Cold War ("Penta-Bonn"). By this time many cartoons indicated Adenauer as dictating policy to the West and, in turn, Hitler's ghost dictating foreign policy to Bonn. The United States was attacked for its intensified rocket building activity not only in Italy, but also in Greece, Turkey, and Great Britain. It was also accused of sabotaging the Geneva disarmament talks. And one cartoon still repeated the accusation that the United States had used bacteriological warfare in Korea and was engaged in the production of chemical weapons (*Izvestia,* June 12, 1959). United States hypocrisy was ridiculed in Fomichev's cartoon in *Izvestia,* of May 29, in which the United States was erecting a monument to the victims of the atomic bomb in Hiroshima.

The rostrum of Western leaders included the West Germans Adenauer, Willy Brandt, Defense Minister Strauss, Foreign Minister von Brentano. An accidental slip, or an open statement of the superiority of the Russian nation over other Soviet nationalities appeared in the *Pravda* cartoon of January 17: the Lunar rocket had "Russian nationality and Soviet citizenship."

Soviet cartoons ignored Vice-President Nixon's visit to the Soviet Union.

The second half of 1959 witnessed a cold war thaw culminating in Khrushchev's September visit to the United States. While official Soviet propaganda played the tune of peaceful coexistence and friendship to audiences abroad, domestically the total number of anti-Western and anti-American cartoons in both papers (but especially in *Izvestia*) exceeded those during the 1958 Berlin and Middle East crises. However, in contrast to other years specifically anti-American cartoons were fewer in number than anti-Western, of which anti-German constituted the single largest group. One possible reason for the generally large number of anti-Western and anti-American cartoons might have been an effort to offset popular Russian expectations that Khrushchev's visit to the United States would result in relaxation of international tension or of domestic vigilance on the part of the Soviet Union.

Izvestia, surpassing *Pravda,* presented 101 cartoons, of which 35 were anti-American (compared with eight in 1958), 47 anti-Western, and 19 praising the Soviet Union. *Pravda* carried 65 cartoons, of which 17 were anti-American (32 in 1958), 38 were anti-Western, and 10 pro-Soviet.

Pravda had 26 cartoons of purely domestic interest and *Izvestia* 32.

Another contrast was the absence of the restraint in anti-American comment that was characteristic of 1955, another period of Cold War thaw. No cartoons unfavorable to the West, in general, or the United States, in particular, had appeared in the period before, during, or after the Geneva summit meeting.

In presenting anti-American cartoons in 1959, however, *Pravda* showed some restraint in anti-American comment, at least until after the visit. *Izvestia* did not.

The largest single group of cartoons during the second half of 1959 were those censuring West Germany. In these Chancellor Adenauer and the newly emerging West German Army were portrayed as successors of Hitler and the Wehrmacht, bent on avenging the losses of World War II. (See Cartoon V-21, below.) *Pravda* carried 13 and *Iz-*

«Г-н Аденауэр, видимо, считает, что теперь западному миру невозможно обойтись без его, аденауэровского, руководства. Не заболел ли манией величия г-н Аденауэр? Очень похоже на то, что произошло именно такое несчастье, и человек, облеченный большой властью в ФРГ, напрягает сейчас все свои силы, чтобы повернуть историю вспять».

(Из речи Н. С. Хрущева на митинге, посвященном дружбе народов Советского Союза и Германской Демократической Республики).

Рисунок Кукрыниксы.

МАНИЯ ВЕЛИЧИЯ.

V-21

MEGALOMANIA
by Kukryniksy

"Mr. Adenauer obviously considers that the Western world cannot now do without his Adenauerish leadership. Hasn't Mr. Adenauer fallen ill with megalomania? It is much like such a misfortune. And a man, revived by great power in the German Federal Republic, now exerts all his strength to turn history backward."
—From N. S. Khrushchev's speech at a meeting devoted to friendship of the peoples of the Soviet Union and the German Democratic Republic.

PRAVDA, June 20, 1959, p. 4

V—22

A SIMPLE MECHANISM
by V. Fomichev

*"Diplomatic hand-brake of the Adenauer-Brentano
System. It operates in the interest of the Cold War."
The wheel reads "Negotiations."*

IZVESTIA, June 4, 1959, p. 1.

vestia 19 cartoons directly related to West Germany, while there were numerous indirect references in other cartoons on more general themes. Topics of some of the anti-German cartoons were: "The Bonn Ditch-Digger"; West German snakes with swastikas in West Berlin (repetition of the symbol used in 1958); Bonn's power politics approach to international relations, (see Cartoon V-22, right); Bonn's strangling of England and France; Adenauer surrounded by Nazi figures shivering at the thought of relaxation in the Cold War. *Izvestia* used similar symbols in a still more unattractive fashion (West German wasps coming out of a swastika nest; the Dusseldorf trial of peace-lovers; Bonn's sabotage of the disarmament talks). A related campaign censured Generalissimo Franco, tying him to the West, NATO, and the United States.

Anti-American sentiments at this time continued to express the tired, overworked topic that the United States is a leader of aggressive military alliances and a nation in which business and military circles are responsible for all warmongering policies. Former Secretary of State Acheson still held the attention of Soviet cartoonists. In one sketch of Kukryniksy on December 6, Acheson and his froglike associates wallowed in the muddy pond of the Cold War. He was similarly portrayed in two additional cartoons. The United States was adorned with the swastika and other Nazi symbols.

Pravda carried nine cartoons attacking American foreign policy and its general warmongering orientation, while *Izvestia* carried thirteen. In addition, there were four cartoons in *Pravda* and eight in *Izvestia* focusing on United States policy in Asia (Laos, Chiang Kai-shek, Japanese militarism); and *Izvestia* added criticisms of SEATO and discussion of the Tibetan question in the United Nations. Nor was United States Middle Eastern policy forgotten: one in *Pravda* and three in *Izvestia* attacked CENTO. The North Atlantic alliance was the central villain in one *Pravda* and seven *Izvestia* cartoons. These concentrated, for example, on the former Wehrmacht general Speidel whose position as Bonn's representative to NATO "proved" the aggressiveness of the alliance and its contamination by erstwhile Nazis.

United States internal inequities received less mention than foreign affairs, with one cartoon in *Pravda* and two in *Izvestia*. "Steel Manufacturer Hits Labor Over the Head—Strike Starts," which *Pravda* took from the *AFL-CIO News,* illustrated Soviet utilization of negative criticism from the West to demonstrate to Russian readers the dissatisfaction of Americans with their lot. *Izvestia* presented one cartoon from the *New York Post* by Bill Mauldin on the Strategic Air Command; its second, a Russian cartoon, disparaged American space failures.

In order to blunt whatever favorable impression might have been created by some of the soliloquies of Khrushchev's trip to the United States, *Pravda* took care to educate its readers ideologically through five cartoons (*Izvestia* had only one) that capitalism in the United States, even the so-called new or "humanitarian" capitalism, remained just as decadent as classical capitalism. Adolph Berle, Jr., author of a book on humanitarian capitalism, was denounced as a fraud, while Marx was said to have indicated the essential similarity of the two types. A cartoon from *L'Humanité* revealed the hidden side of capitalism: the ocean of dullness, the forest of egoism, the lake of unemployment, black pits of decay, the crater of colonialism and the camp of fascism.

Cartoons on disarmament, especially in *Izvestia,* reproached the West for lack of a sincere desire for constructive negotiations. *Pravda* had two, one praising Russia's creative efforts towards disarmament, the other condemning United States recalcitrance. *Izvestia* carried nine, many pointing to West Germany as the main stumbling block to Western acceptance of constructive proposals. In one of the more spirited cartoons on disarmament, that by Fomichev on December 18, in *Izvestia,* Selwyn Lloyd, British Foreign Secretary, was shown favoring disarmament, provided the process

began at the South Pole. To French atomic bomb-testing in the Sahara Desert, *Pravda* devoted two cartoons and *Izvestia* three.

A campaign to save the Greek Communist Manolis Glezos, who was sentenced to death, was the project of three *Pravda* and five *Izvestia* cartoons. One in *Pravda* praised the African and Asian peoples and criticized the colonialists, and eight more in *Pravda* praised the Soviet Union for its space achievements and peace-loving stance. One each in *Pravda* and *Izvestia* commented specifically on Sino-Soviet friendship and another in *Izvestia* acclaimed the Chinese people. *Izvestia* had 17 other cartoons praising the Soviet Union; most dealt with space accomplishments.

With regard to the general conduct of the Cold War, the Soviet papers utilized a number of black-white cartoons. *Pravda* carried five such cartoons and *Izvestia* two. The Soviet icebreaker *Lenin* cracked the ice of the Cold War; socialism was depicted as good, capitalism, bad; Africa's urge for freedom destroyed the colonialists; NATO pushed France to the Sahara for A-bomb tests, while a unified Africa protested "NO!"

Khrushchev's visit to the United States was celebrated in four *Pravda* and six *Izvestia* cartoons. *Pravda* showed the *Lenin* icebreaker (again) and Khrushchev's plane ("Destination: Washington") cutting through the clouds of Cold War. Mickey Mouse and Donald Duck narrated the tale of how Khrushchev was forbidden to visit Disneyland. Another cartoon, commenting on Khrushchev's October trip to Peking, emphasized that the Washington journey was but one of many. *Izvestia* indicated that Khrushchev's visit with Eisenhower was horrifying to the NATO warmongers, chief among whom was Adenauer. The American people welcomed Khrushchev, but the warmongers rudely refused.[4]

A special booklet of cartoons, *Vo Imia Mira* (In the Name of Peace), was prepared and published in 1959 after Khrushchev's visit to emphasize the Soviet desire for relaxation of cold war tensions, peaceful coexistence, and cooperation between East and West and especially between the

United States and the U.S.S.R. Its circulation was 100,000 with cartoons by Abramov of *Pravda* and B. Efimov of *Izvestia*. The title page and a number of cartoons within glorified Khrushchev as peacemaker, as a resolute opponent of the Cold War, and as a prophet proclaiming that the future belongs to communism. (See "In the Name of Peace," "Peace Efforts of N. S. Khrushchev," "The Future Belongs to Communism!" and "Like a Miner.") This marked the first appearance of cartoons praising the Soviet leader. (See Cartoons V-23 & 24, this page.)

V—23

LIKE A MINER
by B. Efimov

Khrushchev as a coal miner destroys the "Cold War."

This cartoon appeared in *PRAVDA* on January 1, 1960, p. 3. Of the thirty-two cartoons in this booklet, six appeared in *IZVESTIA* and seven in *PRAVDA* between July and December 1959.

V—24

THE FUTURE BELONGS TO COMMUNISM!
by B. Efimov

NOT SO LONG AGO: They persecuted for a single word—Communism.
SEPTEMBER, 1959: The word of the No. 1 Communist sounds over America.
The microphones are labeled "U. S. Broadcasting." The briefcase says "McCarthy Commission," and the dog is labeled "FBI."

IN THE NAME OF PEACE, p. 24.

The West was presented in two types of cartoons. Two cartoons, the only two of this type in the entire booklet, for the first time accorded favorable representation to the West: one portrayed East and West shaking hands in a friendly gesture, and the other showed a smiling Uncle Sam waving his hand and saying, "O.K., Nikita." (See Cartoons V-25 & 26, this page.) Cartoons in the second group depicted the West negatively. One of these took its theme from Khrushchev's speech during his subsequent visit to Peking in which he denounced capitalism (see Cartoon V-27, p. 63);

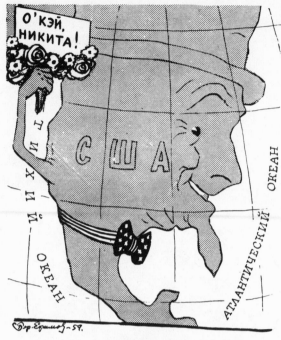

ДЯДЯ СЭМ ДОВОЛЕН ВИЗИТОМ

V—26

UNCLE SAM IS HAPPY WITH THE VISIT
by B. Efimov

Uncle Sam, represented by a roughly geographic picture of the United States and surrounded by the Atlantic and Pacific Oceans, holds a sign reading "O.K. Nikita!"

IN THE NAME OF PEACE, p. 25.

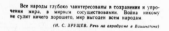

ЖИТЬ В МИРЕ И ДРУЖБЕ!

V—25

TO LIVE IN PEACE AND FRIENDSHIP
by M. Abramov

"All peoples are deeply interested in the preservation and strengthening of peace, in peaceful coexistence. War brings good to no one. Peace is profitable for all peoples."
Khrushchev at the Washington Airport, September, 1959.
The East, holding "peace plans," shakes hands with the West.

IN THE NAME OF PEACE, p. 7.

another, based on Khrushchev's "Social Cosmetics" speech in Novosibirsk, judged "humanitarian capitalism" to be an instrument of capitalist camouflage.

Disarmament supplied the subject for the third group of cartoons. "About Those Who Grieve," taken from the September 24, *Izvestia,* showed representatives of NATO, the Wehrmacht, and business interests, along with Chiang Kai-shek, hiding under a chair—all of them instigators of the Cold War, all plugging their ears to the harmonic melodies of peace. Another black-white cartoon, from *Izvestia* for September 27, "Who Wants Disarmament and Who Wants Destruction?" showed the working people pointing with approval to a placard that read "U.S.S.R. Proposes Full and Complete Disarmament," while a fat producer of military supplies cried "Destruction." In "Two Paths," the West again followed the route leading to war, while Russia chose the road that led to peaceful coexistence, suggested by a strong healthy worker. A cartoon inspired by Khrushchev's speech before the United Nations General Assembly that was entitled "To Protect Peoples from the Fate of a New War," pictured disarmament as the fence that prevented the Cold War from getting out of control.

This same booklet, in discussing general issues of the Cold War, blamed the West for tensions and praised the Soviet Union for its unremitting peace efforts. In the cartoon, "Who Has 'A Dead Rat in His Mouth' and Who Has An Open Heart?", taken from the August 8, *Izvestia*, sweetness and light surrounded the Soviet half of the sketch, while sinister shadows of night darkened the intrigues of Western imperialism. Another, "Don't Look at Others," treated Khrushchev's plea for increased trade between East and West; this time the Cold War was an ugly woman trying to drag her companion (with a dollar sign in his lapel) away from an attractive girl, called "Friendship," who advertised trade with Soviet Russia.

Another speech by Khrushchev, before the National Press Club in Washington, spurred a cartoon on the favorite Soviet theme that Western reporting is inaccurate and increases Cold War tensions. It showed battered pressmen leaving the meeting; they had been unmasked by Khrushchev's attack. Another Khrushchev statement before the United Nations served as the basis for "Harmful Bacilli," with enlargements of the bacilli of cholera, the plague, and the Cold War. (See Cartoon V-28, p. 64.)

One final cartoon, "Frying in the Frying Pan," reprinted from *Izvestia* for October 11, was based on Khrushchev's statement in Moscow after his return from the United States and showed American warmongers flung into the flames of world public opinion.

What is particularly significant about this book-

СОЦИАЛИСТИЧЕСКИЙ КОНЬ
И КАПИТАЛИСТИЧЕСКАЯ КЛЯЧА

V—27

THE SOCIALIST STEED AND THE CAPITALIST NAG
by M. Abramov

"We have challenged the capitalist countries to peaceful competition. As honest partners confident of our own success, I said to my American listeners: 'We warn you. Look, we will inevitably win over you. Why are we so confident about this? Because we are on the right road, we are on a new fresh socialist steed, while you ride on an old capitalist horse. He still carries you, but this is the type of horse which has broken down, limps and trips, so the rider must be on the alert, for otherwise he will be thrown off."
—N. S. Khrushchev. Speech in Peking.

The socialist rider carries the banner "Seven-Year Plan." The capitalist nag is being whipped by a dollar sign.

IN THE NAME OF PEACE, p. 27.

let is that two of its cartoons, one each by Efimov of *Izvestia* and Abramov of *Pravda*, presented the West in a positive (favorable) fashion for the first time, in a *druzheskii sharzh*, which had never before been applied to the opponents but had been reserved for Soviet leaders, prominent scientists, poets, cosmonauts, and other citizens. This was a marked but temporary reversal of policy that was not soon repeated.

It was also noteworthy that many of the cartoons in this booklet appeared in *Pravda* and *Izvestia* between August and November. Only those cartoons appeared in the newspapers that either praised Khrushchev and Soviet peace efforts or blamed the West for its addiction to the Cold War and its opposition to disarmament and cooperation with the Soviet Union.

Noticeable also was the focus of most of the cartoons on Khrushchev's speeches prior to his departure for the United States, during his visit here, upon his return to Moscow, and during his October voyage to Peking. Analysis of the content of his statements reveals a lack of consistency in his supposed pursuit of a policy of peaceful co-existence (see texts of cartoons). In view of the "tough" Chinese position on international relations, Khrushchev's denunciation of the United States in Peking is not difficult to comprehend. But the general tenor of cartoon themes and of Khrushchev's speeches in Russia, both before and after his trip, scarcely reflected an atmosphere of peaceful coexistence. There was no attempt to foster the "spirit of Camp David" and the new era of cooperation. The number of anti-American cartoons in *Pravda* increased following Khrushchev's visit (in comparison with those before or during), and the number was the same in *Izvestia*.

ВРЕДОНОСНЫЕ БАЦИЛЛЫ

V—28

HARMFUL BACILLI
by B. Efimov

"In order that the principles of peaceful co-existence be fully established in relations between states, in our opinion the 'cold war' must be ended. Nations cannot permit such an unnatural state of 'cold war' to continue in the future, just as they cannot allow epidemics of plague and cholera to rage."

—*N. S. Khrushchev at a meeting of the U.N. General Assembly.*

Microscope enlargements of the germs of plague, cholera and cold war are depicted. Note that the cold war germs are dollar signs and swastikas.

IN THE NAME OF PEACE, p. 15.

1960 PARIS SUMMIT CONFERENCE AND THE UNITED NATIONS GENERAL ASSEMBLY SESSION

Because of the proposed Paris conference of the four heads of state, the year 1960 opened with expectations of another period of Cold War thaw similar to that of 1955 after the Geneva conference. But in contrast to 1955, when peace hopes reached a high point, the proposed 1960 Paris summit meeting and the months following were a period of great international tension. As President Eisenhower had dominated the 1955 Geneva talks with his "open skies" proposals for disarmament and inspection, so Premier Khrushchev and his anti-American charges centering on the flight of the U-2 aerial reconnaissance plane over the Soviet Union became the focal point of the press of all countries in 1960. The U-2 episode culminated in Khrushchev's outbursts in New York during the fall session of the United Nations General Assembly.

Reflecting the international tensions of the year, anti-American and anti-Western vituperation in the two Soviet papers reached unparalleled heights in 1960. For the third consecutive year *Izvestia* cartoons on foreign affairs outnumbered *Pravda*. The former averaged one per issue, carrying 296 cartoons in its 300 issues, while *Pravda* had 218 cartoons in 365 issues. *Izvestia* included 209 anti-American cartoons, 70 anti-Western, and 17 that exalted the Soviet Union. *Pravda* carried 171

«РЕВАНШИСТОЗАВР»

АЙСБЕРГ В ВОДАХ АТЛАНТИКИ. (К поездке канцлера ФРГ в США)
Рис. В. Фомичева.

V—30   THE AVENGER
              by V. Fomichev

"Iceberg in Atlantic waters."
Concerning the journey to the U.S.A. by the Chancellor of the German Federal Republic. Adenauer is labeled "Cold War," while his iceberg says "Icy Reserves of International Tension."

IZVESTIA, March 17, 1960, p. 3.

«ВНУТРИАТОМНОЕ СЦЕПЛЕНИЕ»

...новый план создания в Западной Европе «многонациональных мобильных ядерных сил НАТО» предназначен в значительной мере для того, чтобы служить новой формой маскировки ядерного оснащения западногерманских милитаристов и реваншистов.
(Из Заявления ТАСС).

Плоды научных изысканий генерала Норстэда.
Рис. В. Фомичева.

V—29   ATOMIC CHAIN-REACTION
           by V. Fomichev

"nATOM—Its Nucleus and Structure"

"Results of the scientific investigations by General Norstad . . . The new plan for the formation of 'NATO multi-national mobile nuclear forces' in Western Europe is intended to a considerable extent to serve as a new way of concealing atomic armament of the West German militarists and avengers."
The center of the atomic cluster is labeled "Bundeswehr," while Norstad's bomb decorations spell "NATO."

IZVESTIA, March 13, 1960, p. 3.

anti-American, 35 anti-Western, and 28 in praise of the Soviet Union. *Pravda* and *Izvestia* more than tripled their cartoon outputs in comparison with the highest previous number of cartoons (1959, for both papers).

Before the Summit. The following themes were presented by the two Soviet papers in the period from January 1, to May 5, 1960, that is, before the official announcement of the shooting down of the U-2 plane over Russian territory.

Most significant numerically were cartoons on American warmongering and aggressive military and foreign policy, the subject of 13 cartoons in *Pravda* and 28 cartoons in *Izvestia*. The NATO and SEATO alliances were attacked most bitterly, and there was a special attempt to link the United States with its former enemies Germany and Japan, which were portrayed as controlled by their war-

Сергей ВАСИЛЬЕВ ИМПЕРИАЛИСТИЧЕСКАЯ ЯРМАРКА

Пестрое, как водится,
зрелище лабазное.
Оптом тут и в розницу
продается разное.

Разное — бывалое,
сходное с половою,
в основном — лежалое,
далеко не новое.

На поверку — квелое,
кислое, слюнявое,
ржавое, комолое,
затхлое, гунявое.

Что — сто раз подмочено,
что — до дыр захватано,
что — враждой источено,
что — враньем залатано.

Кто — измазан сажею
(хоть в цене возносится!),
кто — протух весь заживо
и на свалку свозится.

Шла б торговля бойкая
у купцов-вонтелей,
не хватает только им,
только... потребителей!

Рисунок М. Абрамова.

V-31

IMPERIALIST MARKET PLACE
by M. Abramov

Lower left: Adenauer is selling the West German army to the Pentagon, saying: "We fattened the pig, just right for the kill."
Top left: U.S. market for spies and diversionists.
Lower middle: Franco trying to sell bases to West Germany.
Middle: A song, "The Good Old Days," is sung by colonialists on crutches.
Top middle: "Avengers" merry-go-round.
Top right: A home for the "aged"—Oberlander, Rhee, etc.
On the stage: "Ensemble of People's Capitalists," singing "We're humanitarian, we're for the people, we're not for the hydrogen bomb!!"
Middle right: Kishi pulls an American on a riksha.
Lower right: U.S. press—lies, slander, etc.

PRAVDA, May 1, 1960, p. 6.

Н А   Ю Г Е   С Ш А

— Я глубоко сожалею об инцидентах в Южно-Африканском Союзе...
Рис. А. Колли

V-32   IN SOUTHERN USA
                by A. Kolli

*"I deeply regret the incidents in the Union of
South Africa. . . ."*

IZVESTIA, April 2, 1960, p. 3.

time militaristic circles. (See Cartoon V-29, p. 65.) Both papers' cartoons noted Adenauer's trip to the United States and his subsequent journey to Tokyo. (See Cartoon V-30, p. 65.) Another supposed link to fascism was discovered in the increasing friendship between West Germany and Franco's Spain, and close United States connections with both. Attention was also focused upon American reluctance to negotiate disarmament agreements, satisfactory to the Soviet Union, as well as upon United States increased military expenditures, encouragement of further French imperialism in Africa, and United States "neocolonialism." (See Cartoon V-31, p. 66.) At the same time one cartoon in *Pravda* and five in *Izvestia* applauded Soviet demobilization of 1.2 million troops as a genuine contribution to peace. It was noted that the West had made no similar moves,

although the fact that Soviet troops still outnumbered Western armies was neglected.

American internal problems were covered exclusively by *Izvestia* which had six cartoons. "In Southern U. S. A." commented on racial problems; the economic plight of the common man received due attention in "Taxes, Taxes"; and the American press was, as usual, attacked, in "Peddler of the Yellow Press." (See Cartoon V-32, this page.)

The second most significant group numerically were those concentrating on the purported Nazi characteristics of West Germany, relating them and similar "fascist" developments to the United States military and ruling circles. (See Cartoon V-33, this page.) *Pravda* had twelve cartoons that were anti-West German in character and *Izvestia,* nineteen. A favorite trick was to confuse, for example, Chancellor Adenauer with Hitler or Defense Minister Strauss with Goering.

Two *Izvestia* cartoons discussed the Common Market. Strife between the Outer Seven and the Inner Six and American interference in Common Market affairs were the contribution of *Izvestia* to this theme which was to assume greater proportions as the European Economic Community increased in significance.

Рисунок М. Абрамова.

Сенатор Голдуотер пикирует...

V-33

SENATOR GOLDWATER DIVES . . .
                by M. Abramov

*Senator Goldwater spits bombs with signs reading:
"Against Peace" and "Against Negotiations."*

PRAVDA, March 21, 1960, p. 3.

Six cartoons in *Izvestia* attacked colonialism and one in *Pravda* the American brand of neo-colonialism. An additional cartoon in each paper commented on Cuban reforms and the elimination of Yankee imperialism.

There were eight cartoons praising the Soviet Union in *Pravda;* two extolled Khrushchev and Lenin (May Day cartoons). Eleven in *Izvestia* included three on Khrushchev's earlier visit to Paris; one portrayed the East-West economic struggle, while others focused on the Soviet Union's blueprint for peace in contrast to Western militarism.

Izvestia cartoons outnumbered those in *Pravda* while covering basically the same themes and often using almost identical drawings. There were only minor variations: Izvestia placed somewhat greater emphasis on colonialism, the Common Market, and carried three cartoons in connection with Khrushchev's March visit to Paris, whereas there had been none in *Pravda* on his trip. In addition both papers, but especially *Izvestia,* in presenting the American domestic scene and issues of racial discrimination and unemployment, relied on cartoons taken from the non-Communist Western press (*New York Herald Tribune, New York Post, AFL-CIO News, The Guardian, The Observer*).

However, the most interesting observation in the period prior to the summit meeting is the contrast between cartoons in this period in 1960 with cartoon preparation for the summit meeting in 1955 (see Table 1).

Some points are immediately apparent. The total number of cartoons, and the number of anti-American cartoons, was much greater in 1959–1960 than it had been in 1955. Whereas anti-American comment and all cartoon comment ceased in both *Pravda* and *Izvestia* prior to the summit meeting in July, 1955, there was no such halt in 1960. There was a considerable decrease in the cartoons in *Pravda* and in its anti-American cartoons, but no similar tendency in *Izvestia*.

Soviet domestic preparations through propaganda for the summit conference in 1960 thus differed from those in 1955. In 1955, by avoiding comment, favorable or unfavorable, in car-

toons pertaining to the meeting of the heads of state (and by including favorable remarks elsewhere throughout the paper) the Soviet Union made known to the population its hopefulness for negotiations. In 1960, however, several months before the shooting down of the U-2 reconnaissance plane, the Soviet domestic propaganda machine failed (particularly in *Izvestia*) to alter in any considerable fashion what had become its standard fare of propaganda through the years 1958 to 1960.

The cartoon performance lends support to the theory that as early as the Baku speech on April 25, 1960 (and possibly even before), Khrushchev had taken a "hard line." Writing in *The New York Times,* Harrison Salisbury observed:

> A quiet shift in the Kremlin has placed the balance of power . . . in the hands of military and political advocates of a harder line toward the West. . . . The shift was carried out in the weeks immediately before May Day and, as the specialists see it, played a major role in Premier Khrushchev's tactics at the summit. . . . The change in the balance of forces occurred before the U-2 plane incident.[5]

During the Summit. The period May 6–31, which included Khrushchev's announcement of the downing of the U-2 plane, the critical 10 days preceding the summit, the few indecisive days in Paris, and the days following the collapse of the Paris talks, was the period of greatest anti-American comment.[6]

On the U-2, specifically, there were 16 cartoons in *Pravda* and 13 in *Izvestia,* while American warmongering, in general, accounted for eight cartoons in *Pravda* and eleven in *Izvestia*. The weary image of Hitler was again put to use. The spying activities of the United States were equated in seriousness with the aggression of the Nazi leader. (See Cartoon V-34, p. 70.) One of the more interesting cartoons, "Confusion at the Pentagon," was of Czech origin. (See Cartoon V-35, p. 70.) It indicated that the Soviet weapon most dangerous to the West is the hammer and sickle, that is, ideology and propaganda.

Table 1.

SOVIET CARTOONS BEFORE 1955 AND 1960 SUMMIT MEETINGS

Months Preceding Summit	PRAVDA 1955			PRAVDA 1959–1960				IZVESTIA 1955			IZVESTIA 1959–1960			
	Monthly Total	Anti-American	Anti-Western	Monthly Total	Anti-American	Anti Western	Pro-Soviet	Monthly Total	Anti-American	Anti-Western	Monthly Total	Anti-American	Anti-Western	Pro-Soviet
7	6	1	5	10	2	3	5	1	0	1	17	5	3	9
6	5	2	3	14	3	8	3	0	0	0	15	6	8	1
5	8	4	4	13	8	5	0	5	3	2	13	5	6	2
4	1	1	0	17	10	4	3	4	2	2	25	14	9	2
3	3	1	2	5	3	2	0	2	1	1	13	6	6	1
2	0	0	0	7	1	5	1	1	0	1	16	7	8	1
1	0	0	0	4	1	3	0	0	0	0	16	8	8	0
7-Month Total	23	9	14	70	28	30	12	13	6	7	115	51	48	16

The seven months prior to the two summits were compared. In 1955 the seven months preceding and including the summit were January–July 1955. The meeting commenced on July 18. While the invitation for the 1955 summit meeting was officially issued on June 18, and the Soviet Union responded on June 18, the matter had been under discussion by the governments concerned since the beginning of the year. For 1960, the seven months prior to the downing of the U-2 plane are listed (October, 1959–April, 1960). In the case of the 1960 summit, the meeting had been agreed to in principle at the Camp David meeting of Eisenhower and Khrushchev in September, 1959. The U-2 incident invalidated further comparison, since the events were no longer comparable.

Izvestia was in this period more sophisticated than *Pravda*. Almost all of its cartoons connected the special case of the U-2 with the broader issue of American warmongering, associating the United States with Nazi (West) Germany or portraying the United States as the leading threat to world peace. (See Cartoons V-36 & 37, p. 71.) Another type of cartoon associated America, Germany, Franco, Kishi, and the U-2 ("Tell Me Who Are Your Friends" and "Football games in Madrid, Washington, Bonn, West Berlin, and Tokyo").

The American domestic scene was the subject of two cartoons in *Pravda* and one in *Izvestia;* two of them dealt with the House Committee on Un-American Activities. Anti-West German cartoons that spliced West Germany and the United States appeared twice in *Pravda* and once in *Izvestia*.

ПЕРЕПОЛОХ В ПЕНТАГОНЕ...

V-35 CONFUSION AT THE PENTAGON
by Milan Koprzhiva (Czechoslavakia)

"General! Here it is. We have succeeded in photographing the most powerful and dangerous Soviet weapon."

PRAVDA, May 23, 1960, p. 1.

Four cartoons familiarly played up the Cold War struggle as one between forthright Russia and the nefarious West ("Communist Brigades of Peace and Capitalist Brigades of Cold War" in *Pravda* and "What's Your Line, Scoundrel?" in *Izvestia*).

There were only three pro-Soviet cartoons in *Pravda* but none in *Izvestia*. Rather than casting glory on Soviet achievements in space, prime attention in cartoons was definitely given to Western aggression. *Izvestia,* which in the past had prominently heralded the peaceful intentions of Khrushchev's trips abroad and had sent him off with best wishes, in this case did not extend any such greetings to Khrushchev in its cartoons.

After the Summit. Cartoons on foreign policy and international relations were as follows:

**V-34   SECRET AND PUBLIC ADVISORS
OF THE STATE DEPARTMENT**
by N. Lisogorsky

A capitalist (leafing through shares of defense plants), a Pentagon general, Adenauer, and the ghost of the Nazi "Wehrmacht" are advisers.
The sign reads: "National policy of the U.S.A.—treachery, aggression, espionage, violation of international law."

PRAVDA, May 23, 1960, p. 3.

"YOU DID WRONG. CONFESS AND SAY: 'I WON'T DO IT ANY MORE.' "
—From N. S. Khrushchev's statement at a press conference in Paris.
by B. Efimov

Damaged plane is marked "U-2 Espionage."

IZVESTIA, May 19, 1960, p. 2.

— Нашкодил — признайся и скажи: «Больше не буду».
(Из заявления Н. С. Хрущева на пресс-конференции в Париже)
Рис. Бор. Ефимова.

V-38

WEST BERLIN'S MAYOR BRANDT: "AS YOU SEE, COMRADESHIP FLOURISHES AMONG US!"
by V. Fomichev

The sign at the left reads "Recruiting for the Bundeswehr—Society of Barrack Comrades." The banners in the center are "Artillery Association, 4th Battery," and "Infantry Society." The right-hand sign reads "Comradely Military Staff."

IZVESTIA, July 3, 1960, p. 3.

Бургомистр Западного Берлина Брандт: Как видите, у нас процветает товарищество!
Рис. В. Фомичева.

V-37

GOVERNMENT POLICY
by V. Fomichev

"Three whales, upon which rests the governmental policy of a certain country."

The words in the whale mouths are "force," "espionage," and "aggression." In Russian the first letters of these three words read "U. . . S. . . A."

IZVESTIA, May 18, 1960, p. 4.

Три кита, на которых зиждется государственная политика, одной страны...
Рис. В. Фомичева.

Table 2.

SOVIET CARTOONS FOLLOWING
THE PARIS CONFERENCE

	Pravda				Izvestia			
	Anti-Ameri-can	Anti-West	Pro-Rus-sian	Total	Anti-Ameri-can	Anti-West	Pro-Rus-sian	Total
June	24	3	1	28	23	2	1	26
July	15	1	–	16	24	3	–	27
Aug.	10	5	4	19	26	5	3	34
Sept.	12	2	3	17	17	3	5	25
Oct.	17	5	3	25	23	7	1	31
Nov.	12	2	4	18	25	3	2	30
Dec.	10	8	5	23	19	5	1	25

Although *Pravda* carried fewer cartoons in each of the six months following the summit and the U-2 in comparison with those published in May (38), *Izvestia* continued to carry the same number or even a larger number in most of the six months after May (28), thus using to maximum advantage the U-2 and the summit collapse to imprint an unfavorable image of the West, and especially of the United States, on the minds of Russian readers. In particular, West Germany had the dubious honor of being replaced by the United States as the leading aggressor and threat to peace. The Nazi symbol was often used to point up this substitution of roles. (See Cartoons V-38, p. 71, and 139, right.)

An innovation of *Pravda* and *Izvestia* cartoonists during this period was the introduction of a long absent figure to the series of Cold Warmongers. The face of President Eisenhower joined those of President Truman, Acheson, Nixon, Dulles, Rockefeller, Pentagon generals, greedy munitions-makers, businessmen, Adenauer, and Franco on the roster of the enemies of socialism. From June to December, *Pravda* carried ten cartoons showing Eisenhower, and *Izvestia* featured

the American President in 15. (See Cartoons V-40, 41, p. 73; 42, & 43, p. 74.)

To the topics of American aggression, treachery, and arrogance towards its allies was added the problem of racial integration in New Orleans to demonstrate that the United States joins the colonialist countries in depriving the Negro of his rights. United Nations intervention in the Congo was portrayed as an American-inspired military operation. In many cartoons United Nations troops were labeled with dollar and pound-sterling signs, leaving the Soviet reader with the impression that American and British forces were employed in the Congo rather than United Nations troops drawn chiefly from African and neutralist nations. (See Cartoon V-44, p. 75.)

На «усиленном питании».   Рис Н. Карповского.

V-39   A "STRENGTH-GIVING DIET."
by N. Karpovsky

"Bonn," with his U.S. knife, French fork and British napkin, is being fed a "Polaris" missile.

IZVESTIA, August 2, 1960, p. 1.

КТО ЧЕМ ИНТЕРЕСУЕТСЯ... (Впечатления из зала суда)

Пауэрс — долларами.   Кардинал Спеллман — шпионскими душами.   Пентагон — системой советской обороны.   Госдепартамент — срывом совещания в верхах.   Белый дом — всем перечисленным и еще гольфом.

Рис. Бор. Ефимова.

V-40

WHAT ARE THEIR INTERESTS?
by B. Efimov

Powers: Dollars.	Cardinal Spellman: The souls of spies.	Pentagon: Defense system of the Soviet Union.	State Department: Wrecking of Summit Meetings	White House: All of these, plus golf.

PRAVDA, August 20, 1960, p. 5.

ЗАЩИТНИК «ПОРАБОЩЕННЫХ СТРАН» И ЕГО ТРИБУНА.   Рисунок М. Абрамова.

V-41

THE DEFENDER OF
"ENSLAVED COUNTRIES"
AND HIS ROSTRUM
by M. Abramov

In one hand President Eisenhower holds a speech entitled "Captive Nations' Week," and in the other, jail keys spelling out "Freedom." The windows of the jail are labeled "Taiwan, Spain, Puerto Rico, South Korea, South Vietnam, the Dominican Republic, and Nicaragua."

PRAVDA, July 22, 1960, p. 5.

In anti-Western cartoons the most prevalent theme was the revamped German militarism, its influence on the policies of the Pentagon, and the menace of West Germany to other countries of Europe. Cartoons employing the black-white technique, juxtaposing the Soviet Union and colonial peoples as good with the West as evil, increased over previous years; again the United States bore the brunt of the criticism. During the 1960 fall session of the United Nations, *Izvestia* again produced a comradely cartoon of Khrushchev, who was depicted as the powerful voice of the millions demanding peace. (See Cartoon VII-6, p. 121.) Other cartoons commemorated Soviet space successes, a suitable topic for the increased number of cartoons praising Soviet achievements. The

United Nations session was amply covered in *Pravda*. Its presentation centered on American aggression and manipulation of the United Nations and on the skulduggery of Secretary-General Dag Hammarskjold.[7]

In their coverage of the fall session of the United Nations General Assembly, *Pravda* and *Izvestia* both presented the Soviet Union as the leader of the forces fighting for the preservation of peace by virtue of its plan for total disarmament; the ugly and clearly labeled United States military officials clung to their schemes for using hydrogen bombs and other lethal weapons (see "Peace," and "Welcome Khrushchev!" in which New Yorkers try to welcome Khrushchev but are prevented by the police and other warmongers).

ОПАСНЫЕ АТОМНЫЕ БОЕГОЛОВКИ...
Рисунок Н. Лисогорского.

V-42

OPPONENTS OF DISARMAMENT . . .
DANGEROUS ATOMIC WARHEADS
by N. Lisogorsky

Eisenhower: "I personally approve of the U-2 flights . . ."
Herter: "I'm for legalization of espionage . . ."
Nixon: "I propose an aggressive policy . . ."
Adenauer: "Hurray for the cold war . . ."
Gates: "I declare a military alert . . ."

PRAVDA, June 14, 1960, p. 3.

Не лезьте, мистер Гертер, — мы сами с усами...
Рисунок Н. Лисогорского.

V-43

DON'T MOVE IN ON US, MR. HERTER,
WE ARE WISE TO YOUR TRICKS.
by N. Lisogorsky

U.S. Secretary of State Herter is showing "Cuba" a sign stating: "I forbid you to make friends with the Soviet Union!"

PRAVDA, September 2, 1960, p. 5.

President Truman in "Silence of Despair" was handled most unceremoniously, and Uncle Sam appeared as a gangster in the cartoon "Afraid of His Shadow." (See Cartoon VII-1, p. 117.) American manipulations in the United Nations provided the focus for the cartoons "And Now Vote" and "U.N. Robot on Duty." Meanwhile *Izvestia* blamed the United Nations and the United States for the turmoil in the Congo ("Behind the Curtain Scene" and "Merry-Go-Round of Imperialism in the U.N.") and the United States for racial segregation in "The U.N.—Entrance for Blacks." (See Cartoon V-45, p. 75.)

The death of Stalin and the subsequent events had no immediate repercussions on cartoons. Cartoon output in the four years 1954 to 1957 was exceptionally low. During the transition of power, old policies were followed. The most common cartoon response in the event of uncertainty was silence—for six months following Stalin's death and during the tentative rapprochement of 1955 —or considered restraint, as in presenting the events of 1956. The Soviet outer space successes in late 1957, Khrushchev's emergence as the undisputed leader, Adzhubei's assumption of the editorship of *Izvestia,* and the Central Committee decrees on *Pravda* and *Izvestia*, all in the period 1957–1959, marked the beginning of a new era in the Soviet press. The dramatic intensification of cartoon attacks against the West and the United

ДРАПИРОВОЧНАЯ РАБОТА

Использование флага ООН в Конго.
V-45   Рис. В. Фомичева.

WORK BEHIND THE CURTAIN
by V. Fomichev

"Use of the U.N. flag in the Congo."

IZVESTIA, September 11, 1960, p. 2.

Хаммаршельдовские гООлуби...

Рис. Вор. ЕФИМОВА.

V-44

HAMMARSKJOLD'S U.N. DOVES
by B. Efimov

The largest dove-plane is marked "To the Congo." The troops in the planes wear dollar signs and pound sterling insignia. They are welcomed by a military man waving a flag labeled "U.N." and holding a portfolio entitled "Interests of the Uranium Companies."

IZVESTIA, August 24, 1960, p. 2.

States in particular began in late 1957, continued through 1958, and reached a climax of almost hysterical proportions in 1960. The image of President Eisenhower, by Khrushchev's own admission a "man of peace," was thoroughly debased. At the same time Khrushchev's rise to power meant the return to cartoon techniques of the Lenin era. Khrushchev was depicted, as Lenin had been (but not Stalin), as the humanitarian figure of superior wisdom, skill, and power, who would propel the Soviet Union to a position of world leadership.

CHAPTER SIX

PERPETUATION OF THE
PROPAGANDA WAR
1961-1964

Pravda and the entire Soviet press daily propagandize the peaceful foreign policy of the Communist Party and the Soviet Government and Lenin's principle of peaceful coexistence, and irately expose the intrigues of warmongers.

PAVEL A. SATIUKOV[1]

The years 1961 to 1964 witnessed events ranging from extreme crisis to a relaxation of international tension that culminated in limited cooperation between East and West. The Congo crisis of 1960–61 continued to smolder, not only in Africa, but also on the diplomatic front and at the United Nations. Its handling by Secretary-General Dag Hammarskjold triggered a most bitter Soviet propaganda attack on the United Nations and on the person and office of the Secretary-General that was clearly visible in cartoons. The invasion of Cuba in the spring of 1961 and the United States-Soviet confrontation of October, 1962, over Soviet missiles in Cuba marked peaks of tension between the two nations. Comment on Cuba and anti-American sentiment, however, were only moderately apparent in Soviet domestic cartoons. The July, 1961, meeting in Vienna between President Kennedy and Premier Khrushchev, the connection of the "hot" line between Moscow and Washington, and the signing, in August, 1963, of the limited nuclear test ban treaty in Moscow all indicated relaxation of the cold war tensions. The last event evoked a rare friendly cartoon response. And finally, on October 15, 1964, the Khrushchev era, as controversial as the man himself, ended as dramatically as and more unexpectedly than it began, by the swift ouster of the man who, in a similar manner, had disposed of many of his rivals from 1953 to 1957.

The deterioration of relations between the Soviet Union and China became increasingly evident in these years, but the Soviet cartoonists exploited the apparent cracks in the Western alliance and were, on the whole, silent on the Soviet problem.

Soviet resumption of nuclear testing in the fall of 1961 ended unilaterally the moratorium on nuclear testing initiated in Geneva in 1959. This major event, quite naturally was not highly publicized in the Soviet press, nor was the erection of the Berlin Wall in August of the same year.

On the other hand, the nationalistic sentiments

Table 3.

ATTENTION SURVEY OF SOVIET CARTOONS IN 1961-1964

Dominant Theme*	Pravda				Izvestia**			
	1961	1962	1963	1964	1961	1962	1963	1964
United Nations and Hammarskjold	14	0	0	0	18	1	0	3
West Germany	27	10	11	16	24	21	30	33
West Berlin	5	3	1	0	17	10	4	2
Common Market	0	3	2	0	10	8	6	3
American Leaders	8	3	0	6	6	1	8	10
United States and NATO Allies	28	34	8	23	49	49	33	51
United States, Cuba and Latin America	6	9	1	7	15	31	18	23
United States and Asia	5	0	2	18	11	5	12	44
Disarmament and Nuclear Tests (focus on U.S.)	1	32	3	0	2	24	9	3
American Internal Scene	9	10	10	5	21	14	25	23
U.S. and Western Press	2	0	1	1	2	1	3	3
General anti-Western	3	5	6	7	5	13	19	11
Colonialism	9	6	4	9	9	7	8	26
Western Capitalism and Imperialism	6	9	0	5	15	10	3	13
22nd Congress CPSU	29	2	3	1	6	0	0	10
Pro-Soviet Comment, Space and miscellaneous	22	40	17	4	6	13	10	7
Totals	174	166	69	102	216	208	188	265

* Each cartoon, often including a variety of themes, was classified in only one category according to that which in the author's estimation was the *dominant* theme.

** *Izvestia* carried 25 cartoons on its front page in 1962, and 40 in both 1961 and 1963, whereas *Pravda* rarely carried front page cartoons. In 1964, *Izvestia* had 113 front page cartoons.

of the nations of Africa, the Middle East, Asia, and Latin America provided Soviet propagandists and cartoonists with a rich source of material for attacking Western colonialism and imperialism. The Twenty-Second Congress of the Communist Party of the Soviet Union and its idyllic program for attaining communism were a prominent part of the domestic propaganda output, although their influence on international relations was small.

The number of cartoons and the sustained attacks on the West and the United States diminished from the level and intensity that followed the U-2 drama of 1960. During the peak year of 1960 *Pravda* had 218 cartoons and *Izvestia* 296; in the next three years *Pravda* carried 174, 166, and 69, and *Izvestia* had 216, 208, and 188. Cartoon attacks from 1960 on were of greater duration than in earlier years of the Cold War, which had been characterized by fluctuations, shorter violent at-

tacks being relieved by longer periods of relative cartoon silence. Also, in the years 1960 to 1964, the variety of themes exceeded that of previous years. This was combined with greater flexibility and sophistication in presentation and the sustained level of attack. A sizeable majority of the cartoons emphasized the threat to peace and to the Soviet Union posed by the West, while a smaller number glorified the successes of the Soviet Union and its people.

DISARMAMENT, NUCLEAR TESTING, AND THE UNITED NATIONS

Soviet cartoons on disarmament, nuclear testing, and the United Nations most clearly demonstrated the link between Soviet foreign policy and cartoon propaganda output.

Игнорируя требование народов взяться за решение вопросов разоружения, западные державы начинают новую серию ядерных испытаний толкая мир к гонке ядерного вооружения и обострению международной напряженности.   **(Из газет).**

VI-1

UNDER DANGEROUS PROTECTION
by Kukryniksy

"Ignoring the demands of the peoples of the world for solution of disarmament questions, Western powers are starting a new series of atomic tests, pushing the world into an atomic armaments race and aggravation of international tension."

The torn piece of paper under the atomic umbrella reads: "disarmament questions."

PRAVDA, March 7, 1962, p. 8.

Под опасной защитой.

Рисунок Кукрыниксы.

Of the numerous themes appearing in Soviet cartoons in 1961, one, disarmament and nuclear testing, was conspicuous for its absence. Although *Pravda* and *Izvestia* had referred to both issues in frequent cartoons in 1959 and 1960, usually condemning Western failure to accept Soviet proposals, only three cartoons mentioned that subject in 1961 (one in *Pravda,* two in *Izvestia).* This paucity is not surprising, since the Soviet Union must have been making advance preparations for the large-scale atomic testing carried out in October, 1961 (in view of the rather long time considered necessary to conceive and implement such tests).

Cartoons on disarmament and nuclear testing increased considerably during 1962 (32 in *Pravda* and 24 in *Izvestia),* and constituted the second largest group of cartoons on any single subject. They were frequently associated with general anti-Western and anti-American comment and particularly condemned United States efforts to obstruct negotiations.[2] The United States and Great Britain were also attacked for their atomic tests on Johnson's Island.[3] (See Cartoon VI-1, p. 78.) "The Mask Is Discarded," by Efimov, which was one of the few Russian cartoons of the late President, condemned President Kennedy for the resumption of nuclear tests. (See Cartoon VI-2, right.) The attention given to nuclear tests was small compared with that devoted to general negotiations on disarmament.[4] *Izvestia* in this vein showed West Germany and the United States as frogmen seeking to sabotage the Geneva disarmament talks (March 16). France's General de Gaulle was singled out for special treatment (*Izvestia,* March 10) for his persistence in developing a French nuclear striking force.

In 1963 the number of cartoons that dealt with disarmament and nuclear testing was relatively small; three in *Pravda* and nine in *Izvestia.* Many were directed at France's General de Gaulle for refusal to sign the nuclear test ban treaty, rather than at the United States and Great Britain. For the first time in Soviet papers, a cartoon praised equally all three countries, the United States, Great Britain, and the Soviet Union, the signatories of the treaty limiting nuclear testing. Efimov's cartoon "A Good Deed" showed both East and West crossing out the deadly atomic cloud. (See Cartoon VI-3, p. 80.) This was reminiscent of the friendly cartoons of Uncle Sam and the West that appeared four years earlier in the booklet *Vo Imia Mira;* but those cartoons did not appear in *Pravda* or *Izvestia.* Even the half-hearted friendly image of the West was short-lived. General Powers, in Efimov's cartoon "Rostrum of a Cannibal" appeared soon after as the traditional negative image of the United States in cartoons discussing dis-

VI-2   THE MASK IS DISCARDED
by B. Efimov

"Once more about the disarmament problem . . ."
This cartoon contains a short article informing Russian readers about President Kennedy's announcement that U.S. nuclear tests would be resumed in the Pacific. Kennedy's bow-tie bears the word "disarmament."

IZVESTIA, March 4, 1962, p. 4.

armament. (See Cartoon VI-4, right.) Disarmament and nuclear testing were not active topics in 1964 cartoons.

Over the four years cartoons on disarmament and nuclear testing featured, among others, Secretary of State Rusk "puffing an atomic pipe"; Uncle Sam and John Bull lighting "atomic cigars"; General de Gaulle stomping out of the disarmament talks; West Germany pushing the button to launch atomic rockets, with the Pentagon general standing helplessly by; and the strong hand of the Soviet government preventing a Pentagon general from sparking an "atomic holocaust." The rich treasury of Russian proverbs supplied the text and theme for the cartoon "As Spring Wins Over Winter, So Will Peace Conquer War." Peace, a healthy worker, held in one hand the symbols of the peaceful uses of the atom, and with the other grasped a deformed military figure whose helmet bore the identifying marks of dollar signs and a skull. Elsewhere, the Western powers hid under an atomic umbrella. *Pravda* also carried a cartoon, from the

Трибуна людоеда.   Рис. Бор. Ефимова.

VI-4   ROSTRUM OF A CANNIBAL
by B. Efimov

General Powers, head of the U.S. Strategic Air Command, testified before the Senate against ratifying the Anglo-American-Soviet treaty banning above-ground tests. The word on the black cloud is "Hiroshima." Powers says: "And I am against this Moscow treaty."

IZVESTIA, August 27, 1963, p. 1.

London *Evening Standard,* in which President Kennedy was the Statue of Liberty, and its torch was an exploding atomic bomb. The range of images was broad and varied, but always unattractive in presenting the United States and the West.

Cartoons also reflected closely Soviet foreign policy toward the United Nations, especially in cartoons directed at the Secretary-General, Dag Hammarskjold. Many such cartoons appeared in the fall of 1960, but the peak was reached in 1961, with ugly attacks on the Secretary-General, and on colonialists and their African stooges. Cartoons accused Hammarskjold most violently for the death of Patrice Lumumba. Two cartoons in February, 1961, "Ablutions of the Secretary-General of the United Nations" and "You Deserve It" illustrate Soviet distortion of Hammarskjold's role

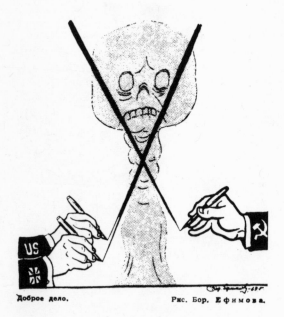

Доброе дело.   Рис. Бор. Ефимова.

VI-3

A GOOD DEED
by B. Efimov

IZVESTIA, August 8, 1963, p. 1.

in the Congo. (See Cartoons VI-5 & 6, pp. 81-82.) In the first cartoon the Secretary-General used bloody knives marked Tshombe and General Mobutu to slaughter Lumumba, and in the second a decadent colonialist in bloody apron gave the Secretary-General a check of eight thousand dollars for his services. These distortions merely continued those started in 1960, which had implied that the United Nations Peace Force in the Congo was composed of American and British troops, rather than its actual composition of Indian, Ghanaian, Ethiopian, and other small neu-

Хаммаршельд действовал в интересах врагов Конго—бельгийских и иных колонизаторов.

(Из заявления Советского правительства в связи с убийством Патриса Лумумбы).

ВЫСЛУЖИЛИСЬ...

Рисунок Кукрыниксы.

VI-5

YOU DESERVE IT
by Kukryniksy

"Hammarskjold worked for the interests of the enemies of the Congo—the Belgians and other colonialists."

—From the statement of the Soviet Government in connection with the murder of Patrice Lumumba.
PRAVDA, February 17, 1961, p. 5.

НЕ СМОЕШЬ!

Даг Хаммаршельд, явля-
ясь фактическим соуча-
стником убийства Лу-
мумбы, сейчас лицемер-
но требует «расследова-
ния» преступления.
                    (Из газет).

Туалет генерального секретаря ООН.   Рис. В. Фомичева.

VI-6   YOU CANNOT CLEAN THEM!
          ABLUTIONS OF THE U.N.
          SECRETARY GENERAL.
               by V. Fomichev

*"Dag Hammarskjold, who actually is an accomplice
to the murder of Lumumba, now hypocritically demands
an 'investigation' of this crime."*
*The towel is labeled "U.N.", the helmet wash-basin
"investigation," and the two bloody daggers "Tshombe"
and "Mobutu."*

IZVESTIA, February 16, 1961, p. 2.

tral nations' troops ("Hammarskjold's U.N. Doves") and that its main purpose, operating behind the United Nations flag, was to protect neo-colonialist interests, and not to restore peace.

The reversal after Hammarskjold's death was abrupt. While in 1961 there were fourteen cartoons in *Pravda* and eighteen in *Izvestia* critical of the United Nations, in 1962 and 1963 only one

appeared, in *Izvestia* in January, 1962. It made the United States responsible for the fate of Antoine Gizenga. No cartoon attacked Secretary-General U Thant. In 1964 the United Nations was mentioned occasionally, but in general terms, and without reference to its specific activities.

ANTI-AMERICAN AND NATO CARTOONS

Of the three general attitudes expressed in cartoons, anti-American, anti-Western, and pro-Russian, the largest proportion of cartoons most often expressed anti-American opinion. The proportion of Soviet cartoons in which the dominant attitude was anti-American often paralleled the shifts in anti-American stance on the part of the Soviet Union. However, cartoons did not reflect apparent Soviet foreign policy toward the United States as clearly as they had Soviet policy on nuclear tests and disarmament and shifts in Soviet attitudes toward the United Nations.

Most of the cartoon themes listed in Table 3 signify anti-American attitudes. One, already discussed because of its special reflection of Soviet foreign policy, was disarmament and nuclear testing. Others dealt with United States aggressiveness through NATO in cooperation with West Germany and other allied powers; the United States, Cuba, and Latin America; the United States and Asia; American leaders (usually referred to in specific contexts and thus discussed under one of the above topics); the evils of the American press—the continuing object of a small number of cartoons; and—a very popular topic—American domestic problems.

Cartoons focusing on the United States and NATO were the most numerous of all categories commenting about the United States. In 1961 they concentrated on American bases abroad, particularly those for nuclear submarines, and on ostensible American and German pressures on Great Britain. The extent of attack ranged even to a shipload of used clothing sent to Turkey that was

VI-7

NATO
by B. Efimov

The American and German sit atop a structure supported by John Bull and a French General. It is composed of letters
reading: "NATO"; top left corner: torch spells "revenge"; colonialist holds a file spelling "Union Minière"; Uncle Sam pours
"kerosine" on the paper reading "peaceful speeches, peaceful statements" to warm the black kettle labeled "Eisenhower-
Dulles Policy." The sack reads "military business"; Franco pours "Valera spirit" to De Valera.

IZVESTIA, May 1, 1961, p. 5.

«США... на словах, например, пекутся о международной безопасности, а посылают (видимо, в порядке «абсолютной дисциплины» в НАТО) в порты своих союзников атомные подводные лодки с «Поларисами», подвергая эти страны и мир смертельной опасности».

(Из ответов Н. С. Хрущева на вопросы директора итальянской газеты «Джорно» И. Пьетра).

Опасный спорт в Средиземном море.
Рис. В. Фомичева.

VI-8

DANGEROUS SPORT IN THE MEDITERRANEAN SEA
by V. Fomichev

"In lip service, for example, the United States is concerned over international security, but (ostensibly under NATO 'absolute discipline') sends atomic submarines with 'Polaris' missiles into the ports of its allies, subjecting these countries and the world to deadly danger."
—From N. S. Khrushchev's answers to questions from an Italian newspaper editor.
The name of the submarine is "Sam Houston."

IZVESTIA, May 10, 1963, p. 2.

presented as an example of American imperialist penetration! (*Izvestia,* July 25, 1961). The 1961 May Day cartoons exemplified the multiplicity of themes presented to Soviet readers on such occasions. Abramov's "Imperialist Hospital" (*Pravda*) and Efimov's "NATO" (*Izvestia*) pictured the United States and West Germany dominating their weaker partners, England and France. Efimov focused on United States warmongering: Uncle Sam poured kerosene while Eisenhower, Truman, Nixon, and United States businessmen warmed their hands at the fires of the Cold War. (See Cartoon VI-7, p. 83.) The other events of the year

(the Eichmann trial; Nazis at large in West Germany; Hammarskjold's cooperation with Belgian colonialists; the Algerian national liberation struggle; Pentagon support for shaky reactionary governments; and Franco's domestic problems in Spain) all received mention in this complicated cartoon.

VI-9

THE DEVIL'S BRIDGE, OR THE PENTAGON'S ILLUSTRATIONS FOR THE WASHINGTON DECLARATIONS
by V. Fomichev

"Desiring to aggravate the international situation, the American military establishment has made a demonstrative gesture, by undertaking an air transfer of soldiers from the U.S.A. to West Germany."
The troops are landing in the German Federal Republic.

IZVESTIA, October 27, 1963, p. 1.

Желая обострить международную обстановку, американская военщина сделала демонстративный жест — предприняла переброску по воздуху солдат из США в Западную Германию. (Из газет).

Чертов мост, или пентагонская иллюстрация к вашингтонским декларациям.
Рис. В. Фомичева.

НОВОСТИ ИЗ-ЗА ГРАНИЦЫ

От зарубежных корр. «Известий» и ТАСС

ПРИВЕТ «ВЫПУСКУ МИРА» В УНИВЕРСИТЕТЕ НАТАЛА

СОТРУДНИЧЕСТВО СССР И ИНДИИ

САМОЛЕТ-АГРЕССОР. НОВЫЕ ПРОВОКАЦИИ ПЕНТАГОНА

ВИЛЬСОН ОСУЖДАЕТ СДЕЛКУ С США

Еще один вариант раздела Кипра

Студенты Леопольдвиля воздвигают баррикады

«Атлас» не поднялся

Корабли 6-го американского флота, прибывшие с «визитом вежливости» в Стамбул, пройдут через Дарданеллы в сопровождении соединения турецкого флота. Эти фактически военные маневры грубо нарушают международную конвенцию о режиме плавания в проливах, подписанную в Монтре.   (Из газет).

Широкое гостеприимство в узких проливах...

Рис. В. Фомичева.

VI-10   BROAD HOSPITALITY IN NARROW STRAITS
by V. Fomichev

"Ships of the American Sixth Fleet, which have come to Istanbul on a "courtesy call,' are passing through the Dardanelles accompanied by units of the Turkish navy. These actual naval maneuvers grossly violate the Montreux international convention concerning the rules for navigation in these straits."

The fish is labeled "Sixth Fleet," while the welcoming Turk is standing on the "Montreux Convention."

This is a typical foreign news index appearing on the front page of Izvestia where, aside from cartoon comment, other headlines resemble the period of American Yellow Journalism.

Other headlines read:
"Greetings to the 'Graduating Class of Peace' at Natal University."
"Cooperation of the USSR and India."
"Airplane—Aggressor. New Provocations by the Pentagon."
"Wilson Condemns a Deal With the USA."
"One More Plan for the Subdivision of Cyprus."
"Leopoldville Students Build Barricades."
" 'Atlas' Firing Delayed."

IZVESTIA, March 11, 1964, p. 1.

ПРЕДОСТЕРЕГАЮЩАЯ ДАТА.   Рисунок Кукрыниксы,

VI-11

A DAY OF WARNING
by Kukryniksy

U.S. officer labeled "Pentagon" looks at Hitler in a noose spelling "May 9"—the date of the German surrender in World War II.

PRAVDA, May 10, 1962, p. 3.

The Kennedy-Khrushchev meeting in Vienna, June 5–6, 1961, produced an interesting result in cartoons. Prior to the meeting both *Pravda* and *Izvestia* ceased printing cartoons against the United States. *Pravda* had no anti-American cartoons from May 1 until June 22, despite the recentness of the Cuban invasion attempt, and *Izvestia* had no specifically anti-American cartoons between May 12 and July 4. Anti-Western sentiment, however, was strong. *Pravda* had two anti-Western cartoons before the meeting (May 5, June 4) and three following the meeting, and *Izvestia* presented a British cartoon on the meeting of Macmillan, Adenauer, and de Gaulle, and eleven other anti-

Western comments before the Kennedy-Khrushchev meeting, and seven following it.

Richer variations appeared in the anti-American and anti-NATO cartoons of 1962. More attention was paid to the threat to world peace posed by the United States. The U.S. Sixth and Seventh fleets reappeared as symbols of aggression. German control over American military decisions was emphasized (*Pravda*, May 19). The Pentagon's dangerous meddling in international affairs—illustrated as throwing lighted torches while standing on a powder keg (*Pravda*, May 22)—revealed its true character as a messenger of death (*Pravda*, April 10, July 22).

In 1963, Soviet hostility in cartoons toward the NATO alliance dropped somewhat in numbers and as a proportion of the total number of cartoons. West Germany remained the keystone of NATO, although there was uncertainty as to which nation represented the greater threat: some cartoons showed the United States giving orders to the Germans, while others showed the Germans domi-

Команда НАТО тренируется.
Рисунок народного художника РСФСР Ю. Ганфа.

VI-12

TRAINING OF THE NATO COMMAND
by IU. Ganf

The basketball board reads: "Revenge;" the German soldier's sweat-shirt: "Bundeswehr."

PRAVDA, July 31, 1964, p. 6.

nating the Americans. Polaris submarines remained a target of cartoon attack that focused in 1963 upon the operation of submarines in the Mediterranean and the consequent danger to Greece and Turkey, as in "Dangerous Sport in the Mediterranean," inspired by Khrushchev's statement. (See Cartoon VI-8, p. 84.) "The Devil's Bridge," considered the American exercise airlift of an entire division from Texas into West Germany as provocative. (See Cartoon VI-9, p. 84.) In 1964, references to NATO resumed their high pitch, with special emphasis on differences of opinion among the NATO allies. (See Cartoons VI-10, p. 85; 11 & 12, p. 86.)

American leaders, especially Presidents Truman and Eisenhower, and to a lesser extent Presidents Kennedy and Johnson, received star billing in critical cartoons. On the eve of his departure from the White House, Eisenhower received prominent mention in Soviet cartoons. On January 6, 1961, he appeared in *Pravda* in military uniform, calling for aggression. *Izvestia* on January 7 presented him as a magician—atomic bomb in one hand, golf club in the other. "It won't work . . ." showed him reaching for Cuba on the map. (See Cartoon VI-13, above.)

Но пасаран! Не пройдут!

Рисунок Н. Лисогорского.

VI-13

"BUT TRAVELER! IT WON'T WORK!"
by N. Lisogorsky

PRAVDA, January 11, 1961, p. 4.

Зарубежная печать не скрывает, что в ходе бесед Кеннеди с Эйзен-
хауэром, Никсоном и Трумэном обсуждались планы подготовки новой агрессии против Кубы. В столицу США слетелась стая бывших президентов и
вице-президентов и раскаркалась, как воронье...   (Из газет).

РАСКАРКАЛИСЬ...   Рисунок Кукрыниксы.

VI-14

THEY CROAKED
by Kukryniksy

*"The foreign press does not conceal that Kennedy's conversations with Eisenhower, Nixon, and Truman
discussed plans for preparation of a new aggression against Cuba. A flock of former presidents and
vice-presidents flew to Washington and croaked like ravens."*
The island is labeled "Cuba" with its port of "Havana."   PRAVDA, April 30, 1961, p. 5.

Cartoonists seemed hesitant to link President Kennedy to the actual invasion of Cuba. "Uncle Sam and the 'Consultants' On the Cold War" by Kukryniksy, in *Pravda* of April 25, 1961, showed Truman and Eisenhower, with snake tongues, advising Uncle Sam on Cuba. The *Pravda* cartoon of April 20 associated Allen Dulles and Eisenhower with the Cuban invasion (but not Kennedy) under the title " 'Freedom' According to the Recipe of Dulles and Eisenhower." Another typical cartoon was that by Kukryniksy, "They croaked. . . ." (See Cartoon VI-14, p. 88.)

President Kennedy was depicted only occasionally by Soviet cartoonists, and then only rarely was his face shown. He appeared more often through reprints of foreign cartoons. A cartoon taken from the *Daily Worker* of London connected Kennedy's New Frontier policy with the policies of Adenauer toward East Germany ("Toward New Frontiers—Drang Nach Osten," in *Pravda* of August 25, 1961). Kennedy's support of West Germany through the provision of small scale nuclear weapons was decried in a reprint of Franklin's cartoon from the London *Daily Mirror* (*Izvestia*, December 5, 1961).

In 1962 there were only two cartoons picturing President Kennedy, both in connection with the resumption of nuclear testing. Efimov's March 4 cartoon ridiculed the "deafness" of the American President and showed him wearing a capitalist top hat. Despite Kennedy's aversion to wearing hats, Efimov repeated that detail, in "Salvaged Banner," where the President greeted the Bay of Pigs prisoners in Miami. (See Cartoon VI-15, right.) The second 1962 cartoon of President Kennedy appeared in *Pravda* and was a reprint from the London *Evening Standard,* in which he symbolized the Statue of Liberty and the torch of freedom was an exploding atomic bomb. In 1963 he also appeared only twice, in January to greet the Cuban prisoners as noted above, and on June 30 in *Izvestia* in a reprint from *Die Welt*. Although Lyndon Johnson received cartoon coverage when he went to West Berlin as Vice-President in August 1961, he did not appear in Soviet cartoons during the

VI-15

"SALVAGED BANNER" OF
THE CUBAN COUNTERREVOLUTIONARIES
by B. Efimov

This front page cartoon accompanied a three column story describing the welcome which President Kennedy and his wife gave to returning "Bay of Pigs" prisoners in Miami. Note Mrs. Kennedy's skirt with dollar signs.

IZVESTIA, January 6, 1963, p. 1.

initial period of his presidency. (See Cartoon VI-32, p. 99.)

Soviet reluctance to depict the American president in office stood in contrast to the frequent abuse given former Presidents Truman and Eisenhower, and Vice-President Nixon. "Eisenhower and the Troika System" showed Eisenhower, again with golf clubs, driving a carriage marked "U.N." (*Pravda,* October 1, 1961). This was based on Kennedy's criticism of the troika plan[5] as unworkable. The incursion of a U-2 plane over a corner of Soviet territory in August, 1962, was the cue for a *Pravda* cartoon on September 6, identifying General Eisenhower as an instructor at

Многие участники совещания ОАГ поддержали антикубинскую позицию Вашингтона в расчете на американскую помощь.
(Из газет).

САНКЦИИ ПРОТИВ КУБЫ

Под дулом банковских сейфов США.   Рис. Ю. Кершина.

VI-16

FACING THE MUZZLE OF THE UNITED STATES BANK VAULTS
by IU. Kershin

"Many participants of the OAS meeting supported Washington's anti-Cuban position bearing in mind American aid."
The sign on the vault reads: "Sanctions against Cuba."

IZVESTIA, August 1, 1964, p. 1.

the school for U-2 pilots. The curriculum included espionage, violation of national borders, and treachery.

President Eisenhower appeared for the first time in Soviet cartoons only after the storm caused by the U-2 incident. His previous appearances, in the late forties as a general plotting against the Soviet Union, were associated with his role as Chief of Staff. (See Cartoon IV-1, p. 25.) The favorable image of President Eisenhower in the Soviet Union was based on his role as Supreme Allied Commander during World War II, and was furthered at the height of the Soviet-Western thaw in 1955 during and following the Geneva talks. His reputation was enhanced by Khrushchev, who presented Eisenhower as a man of peace after he returned from his visit to the United States in 1959. He extended an invitation to Eisenhower to return the visit. The motives for Khrushchev's policy were, no doubt, complex; but for one or more reasons it was destined to be reversed. Following

the U-2 incident in 1960, and continuing throughout 1964, Eisenhower was a frequent target of cartoon attack. In a press where daily, weekly, and monthly plans specify themes in advance, the anti-Eisenhower campaign was not accidental but part of the directed information process.

Cuba and Latin America constituted a relatively new theme that became the subject of growing attention in newspaper articles and cartoons in 1961–1964. (See Cartoons VI-16, above; 17 & 18, p. 91.) The cartoons depicted the United States in the most sinister of aggressive and exploitative roles. The miscarriage of the Bay of Pigs invasion in 1961 was ridiculed in the *Pravda* cartoon of July 28 that showed a strong healthy Cuban shoveling out the muddy remnants of the invading forces. Kukryniksy's comment on American "aid" to Latin America emphasized the dangers of such assistance (*Pravda*, June 10, 1961). Efimov assailed United States intrigues in Latin America and Cuba and threats of military force (*Izvestia*,

НА ВОРЕ ПАНАМА ГОРИТ!
Русская пословица на заморский лад...
Рис. В. Фомичева.

VI-17

THE THIEF'S PANAMA HAT IS BURNING!
by V. Fomichev

"A Russian proverb on overseas harmony . . ."
The proverb under reference states that a thief reveals himself by burning his hat. The cartoon indicates a "Panama" hat burning on the head of the U.S.A.

IZVESTIA, January 19, 1964, p. 1.

ЧИТАЯ РЕЧЬ Н. С. ХРУЩЕВА

Рис. Бор. Ефимова.

VI-18   READING THE SPEECH OF N. S. KHRUSHCHEV
by B. Efimov

The first cartoon pokes fun at Western economists for their statements concerning the slow rate of growth of the Soviet economy. The second laughs at American accusations that Castro stirred up the Panama crisis, especially as he is hunting in the Soviet Union. The third represents Soviet exposure of French militarists.

IZVESTIA, January 21, 1964, p. 1.

VI-19   **U.S. SEVENTH FLEET**
by B. Efimov

*Chiang Kai-shek calls for invasion of the People's
Republic of China.*

IZVESTIA, July 7, 1962, p. 2.

August 28, 1961). A cartoon ridiculed American
policy at the meeting of the Organization of American States which excluded Cuba from the councils
of the organization (*Izvestia,* February 16, 1962).
To this action a robust Cuban replied defiantly,
"I exclude your exclusion, sir!"

All in all, however, relatively little propaganda
capital was made of the Bay of Pigs invasion at
the time. Through April and May of 1961, only
five cartoons appeared on the subject in *Pravda,*
and four in *Izvestia.* These were concentrated in
the period April 18 to May 5. Thereafter followed
a period of silence on these topics which lasted
until well after the meeting of Kennedy and
Khrushchev.

Another significant cartoon pattern was evident
during the last three months of 1962. The United

States blockade of Cuba, in response to Soviet
shipment of rockets with atomic warheads, and the
subsequent crisis through October and November,
illustrated clearly the flexibility of the cartoon.
Starting on October 24, 1962, *Izvestia* expanded
the scope of its anti-American cartoon campaign.

Костюм Макнамары для поездки
в Сайгон.
Рисунок Кукрыниксы.

VI-20

**McNAMARA'S COSTUME FOR
HIS TRIP TO SAIGON**
by Kukryniksy

*"American imperialism and its supporter, the Saigon
clique, are suffering one defeat after another in South
Vietnam. The torturers don't feel safe even in Saigon
itself. Under such circumstances U.S. Defense Secretary
McNamara is being sent to South Vietnam. The purpose
of his visit is to draft new plans to suppress the
struggle of the Vietnamese people for national
liberation."*

PRAVDA, March 5, 1964, p. 3.

From that day through October 28, for five consecutive days, cartoons defending Cuba and condemning the United States for aggression and piracy added their weight to the news, pictures, and editorial statements of the same nature. Then, following Premier Khrushchev's statement confirming the presence of Soviet missiles in Cuba and promising their early withdrawal, cartoon comment on Cuba or directly against the United States suddenly ceased. This policy of silence was maintained throughout November and the first half of December in both papers.

This did not mean cessation of all cartoons. While *Pravda* carried a very small number of cartoons during the one and a half month period (primarily glorifying the Soviet Union), *Izvestia* carried a larger number. They were anti-German, anti-Western, and on capitalism and imperialism generally. The only two cartoons on colonialism (*Izvestia,* November 30, 1962, and *Pravda,* December 1, 1962) singled out colonialism in Africa specifically instead of the usual trio—Asia, Africa, and Latin America.

By mid-December, 1962, the standard themes —the Pentagon's aggressiveness, the lack of freedom in the United States, and mistreatment of Negroes and American communists, American domination of Great Britain (in this case by cancellation of the Skybolt missile program)—returned to the pages of *Pravda* and even more noticeably to those of *Izvestia.* A small cartoon condemning the Cuban blockade supported the general Soviet characterization of the United States as an aggressive country which, by attempting to bury the Soviet Union, would itself be buried (*Izvestia,* December 13, 1962). This was a version of Khrushchev's famous "We will bury you" statement. Comment continued through 1963. The Alliance for Progress appeared in cartoons on Latin America: "Alliance for Progress—A Big Stick of the Washington Virtuoso," (*Izvestia,* March 20, 1963, and August 17, 1963). Cartoons condemned pirate raids on Cuban shipping, the role of the United Fruit Company in Guatemala, and the lack of democracy in Betancourt's Venezuela.

Патроны—американские, мушка — из южновьетнамских гадов.
Рис. В. Черникова

VI-21   AMERICAN CARTRIDGES,
SOUTH-VIETNAMESE GUN-SIGHT
by V. Chernikov

Gun-sight is labeled: "Khanh."

IZVESTIA, June 9, 1964, p. 2.

Until 1964 the role of the United States in Asia received much less attention than Latin America or Cuba in 1961–1962. Cartoons noted the aggressive role of the Seventh Fleet in support of Chiang Kai-shek and Laos, and the implications of American "intervention" in South Vietnam. (See Cartoons VI-19 & 20, p. 92.) Many cartoons noted Asian events in connection with other topics. "Playing With Fire" (*Pravda,* May 22, 1962) by Kukryniksy showed a Pentagon figure clad in dollars, standing atop a powder keg and brandishing torches labeled "American Adventure in Laos," "Interference in Cuban Affairs," "U.S.A. Atomic Tests," and "Provocation in West Berlin." In 1963–1964, however, the progressive deterioration of the situation in Asia, heightened by North Vietnam raids on American ships and retaliatory

ТРАНЗИСТОРЫ МИСТЕРА МЭРРОУ

Рис. Б. Ефимова.

Эдвард Мэрроу занимает видное положение в правительственном аппарате Соединенных Штатов Пусть никого не смутит скромное наименование учреждения, которое он возглавляет. За невинной вывеской информационного агентства США, этого пропагандистского придатка госдепартамента, скрывается гигантский синдикат лжи, протянувший свои щупальца во все концы земного шара.

Мистер Мэрроу сознает трудности, которые стоят перед ним и его агентством. Не так-то просто выдать черное за белое, не так-то легко представить политику усиления опасности войны действиями, направленными на укрепление мира, политику сохранения колониализма — защитой свободы. Каждый внешнеполитический провал Вашингтона, а они следуют друг за другом с точностью часового механизма, наносит удар по без того подмоченному престижу Соединенных Штатов. И за каждый провал приходится расплачиваться Мэрроу, как не сумевшему обеспечить «прикрывающей версией» очередной агрессивный шаг своих хозяев.

Роль «мальчика для битья», судя по всему, порядком наскучила директору информационного агентства. В последнем номере журнала «Тичерс колледж рекорд», издаваемого Колумбийским университетом, он сделал попытку снять с себя обвинения в том, что его ведомству не удается привлечь симпатии народов к американской политике. Из хилого досье аргументов, которыми пользуются в Вашингтоне, чтобы одурачить общественное мнение, Мэрроу вытащил самый подержанный. Пропагандист-

ские неудачи США он, разумеется, объяснил «интригами коммунистов», не ведая, видимо, что тем самым лишний раз признал притягательность идей марксизма-ленинизма для трудящихся всего мира.

Шеф американской пропаганды предложил смелый план пресечения «коммунистических козней». Свои предложения Мэрроу высказал сперва в журнале, а затем повторил их в телевизионном интервью сенатору Кефоверу, что, несомненно, исключает всякое предположение о незрелых и скоропалительных умозаключениях директора информационного агентства США. План Мэрроу донельзя прост и конкретен. Чтобы положить конец принявшим массовый характер издевкам над американской политикой и вытащить престиж Соединенных Штатов из ямы, необходимо, оказывается, совсем немногое. Надо только поднажать на производство транзисторных радиоприемников, увеличить издание книг, распространяемых за рубежом, и расширить сеть заграничных библиотек США, что-де даст другим странам «лучшее понимание и оценку значения Америки».

Мэрроу смотрит в корень вещей, хотя и под особым углом зрения. «Создание радиоприемников на транзисторах — одно из самых важных событий нынешнего столетия», — заявляет он. Нет, не потому, что это новый шаг в развитии науки и техники, позволяющий облегчить и улучшить жизнь людей. «Их создание означает, что сейчас можно общаться по радио с людьми, которые неграмотны, которые не имеют электроэнергии и не имеют эконо-

мики». Вот для чего понадобилось директору информационного агентства «выдающееся открытие столетия»! Ему наплевать, что по милости колонизаторов миллионы людей обречены на нищету, что они не умеют читать и писать. Ему лишь бы заставить их усвоить «американские идеи» и «оценить» значение Америки.

Ну что ж. Будем надеяться, что осуществление плана Мэрроу действительно поможет людям лучше «оценить» значение Америки. Ведь сравнение пропагандистских потуг директора информационного агентства США с конкретными действиями Соединенных Штатов предоставит отличную возможность даже самым доверчивым людям избавиться от последних иллюзий в отношении американской политики. Принесет своеобразную пользу и создание новых американских библиотек за границей. Существование их уже содействовало выявлению общественного мнения о пропаганде, расточаемой этими центрами дезинформации. В связи с этим уместно напомнить мистеру Мэрроу краткое, но исчерпывающе ясное мнение известного американского журналиста Джозефа Олсопа по поводу деятельности его ведомства:

«В старину сигналы о грозящем бедствии, — писал он, — подавались при помощи костров, зажигаемых на вершинах холмов. Теперь предостерегающим сигналом являются полыхающие библиотеки информационной службы США».

Создается впечатление, что Эдвард Мэрроу не склонен прислушаться к этому предостережению. Он намерен подбросить в костер народного гнева против агрессивной политики Соединенных Штатов новую порцию горючего материала. Не будем сожалеть об этом.

Вал. ЛЕДНЕВ.

Прислушивайтесь не к свисту бича, а к «Голосу Америки».

VI-22

TRANSISTORS OF MR. MURROW
by B. Efimov

"Don't listen for the sound of the whip, listen to the Voice of America."

IZVESTIA, February 23, 1962, p. 5

bombing missions, captured more attention. One cartoon commented bitterly that Americans supply the ammunition while South Vietnamese soldiers supply their lives. (See Cartoon VI-21, p. 93.) South Vietnam leaders were presented, as the Koreans, Japanese, and Nationalist Chinese before them, as the puppets of American intrigues.

The Middle East was often touched upon in cartoons on other subjects. Cartoons on NATO often included the Middle East, where the Sixth Fleet symbolized American imperialism. Abramov used a boat with handcuffs to portray the Sixth Fleet (*Pravda,* April 6, 1962). Efimov (*Izvestia,* January 29, 1964) featured Senator Keating threatening Arab countries on behalf of Israel.

The United States communication media, especially the press, were not neglected by Soviet propaganda. Although the number of such cartoons was small, they appeared with consistency in almost every year of the Cold War. "Transistors of Mr. Murrow" and "The Peace Corps" attacked

«Корпус» и его конечности. Рис. Бор. Ефимова

VI-23

THE PEACE CORPS
by B. Efimov

" 'The Corpus' and its extremities."

IZVESTIA, April 25, 1961, p. 1.

American propaganda tactics. (See Cartoons VI-22 & 23, p. 94.) American television was depicted as a weapon of fear; it warned that "the spy is among you" and caused husband and wife to view each other with suspicion (*Izvestia,* January 24, 1961). Moscow utilized the *Der Spiegel* case in Germany to emphasize censorship and restraints on freedom of expression in the West. *Newsweek, Time, Life,* and *Look* were often singled out for attack, as in "Time and Life—

В США снова произведены аресты участников «рейсов свободы». **(Из газет).**

— Вы стремитесь к свободе! Мы отправим вас прямым рейсом!
Рис. Ю. Иванова.

VI-25 "FREEDOM RIDERS" ARE AGAIN BEING ARRESTED IN THE U.S.A.
by IU. Ivanov

"You are trying to attain freedom? We will give you a direct ride!"
The poster reads "Freedom Ride."

PRAVDA, July 28, 1961, p. 5.

VI-24

A SHAMEFUL FACT
by V. Fomichev

"The level of unemployment among Indians amounts to 50 percent and in some cases attains 85 percent. Only 10 percent of Indian housing satisfies the most minimum standards. The average length of life of an Indian is 20 years less than the national average."

—From the conversation of U.S. President Johnson with American Indian leaders.

The brief poem states that Hiawatha is a victim of Wall Street. Below the U.S. seal is a sign, "Indian Reservation." The feathers in the Indian's headdress read: "Hunger," "Poverty," "Unemployment," and "High Death Rate."

IZVESTIA, January 25, 1964, p. 1.

Voices of the Cold War" (*Izvestia,* February 26, 1964).

Comment on American domestic developments was frequent. Reprints of American cartoons critical of unemployment and racial problems by Herblock, Mauldin, and other noted American cartoonists appeared. Herblock's cartoon labeled "The Product of the Western Way of Life" *(Pravda,* January 26, 1962) featured racists, gangsters, and the Ku Klux Klan.

Soviet cartoonists did not neglect racial inequality, lack of political freedom, economic misery, and unemployment. The high mortality rate of American Indians was featured in "A Shameful Fact."

Рисунок Кукрыниксы.

VI-26

SOMETHING LIKE AN EARTHQUAKE SHOOK THE STOCK MARKET
by Kukryniksy

The building is labeled "Stock Market," while the skull is marked "Crisis."

PRAVDA, June 1, 1962, p. 5.

VI-27

THEIR ROOTS ARE THE SAME . . .
by M. Abramov

The figure on the right carries the sign "Democratic Candidate" and the other "Republican Candidate."

PRAVDA, March 18, 1962, p. 3.

(See Cartoon VI-24, p. 95.) The arrests of "Freedom Riders" was but one of many cartoons on that topic. (See Cartoon VI-25, p. 95.) Suppression of the Communist Party in the United States was contrasted to the freedom accorded the Nazi Party (*Izvestia*, February 4, 1962). The nosedive taken by the stock market did not pass unnoticed ("The Stock Market Crash"). (See Cartoon VI-26, p. 96.) Congressional elections in 1962 prompted both papers to point to the essential identity of the Republican and Democratic parties; both were equally tools of Wall Street capitalism ("Their Roots are the Same"). (See Cartoon VI-27, above.) The presidential campaign of 1964, not surprisingly, centered on Senator Goldwater. He was vociferously attacked as a fascist warmonger. His most extreme statements

were illustrated in cartoons. One of the first color cartoons in *Izvestia,* which came into use in June, 1964, showed a swastika whip controlling the GOP elephant. (See Cartoon VI-28, below.) A Herblock cartoon of Goldwater also appeared.

The assassination of President Kennedy in November, 1963, was attributed to rightist elements. "TEXAS," an *Izvestia* cartoon, depicted that state as a haven for "racists, murderers, and lynchers."

— Голосуйте за Голдуотера! — надсадно кричат сторонники «бешеного» сенатора. — Остановите аризонского безумца! — требует большинство американцев. Художник Б. Ефимов в своей карикатуре изобразил предвыборную чехарду в США.

VI-28

VOTE FOR GOLDWATER!
by B. Efimov

" 'Vote for Goldwater!' scream the supporters of the 'mad' Senator."
" 'Stop the Arizona maniac!' demand the majority of Americans."
"The artist Boris Efimov described the pre-election leap-froging in the USA in his cartoon."

IZVESTIA, June 14, 1964, p. 1—color.

TEXAS   VI-29
by Carot (Liberation, Paris)

" 'Here freedom exists only for racists, murderers, and lynchers. This land is the kingdom of lawlessness, tyranny, and force. Such is Texas—the site of the monstrous crime that shook the entire world.' This was the comment of the French artist Carot in the newspaper Liberation on the events connected with the murder of U.S. President John Kennedy."

PRAVDA, November 29, 1963, p. 2.

Свобода существует здесь только для расистов, убийц и линчевателей. Эта земля — царство беззакония, произвола и насилия. Таков Техас—место, где произошло чудовищное преступление, потрясшее весь мир. Так прокомментировал французский художник Каро в газете «Либерасьон» события, связанные с убийством президента США Джона Кеннеди.

(See Cartoon VI-29, above.) This paralleled the interpretation of Kennedy's death which was offered in news stories.

ANTI-GERMAN AND WEST BERLIN CARTOONS

Cartoons reviled West Germany in part as a NATO ally, but more as the heir of the features of Hitler's Nazi Germany: militarism, expansion to the East, arrogance, and cruelty. Barbs attacked the sinister statesmanship of its leaders, Christian Democrats Adenauer and Erhard or Socialist Willy Brandt alike.

Cartoons reiterated the accusation that West Berlin was a Western spy center maintained by Uncle Sam and the German revengers Adenauer, Brandt, and Strauss for the subversion of the socialist countries. The main purpose appeared to

Границу закрыли — хвост волку отрубили...

Рис. Бор. Ефимова.

VI-30   WHEN THE BARRIER FELL—
IT CUT THE WOLF'S TAIL
by B. Efimov

The sign reads: "The Border of German Democratic Republic is closed to all enemies."

IZVESTIA, June 6, 1963, p. 2.

be the justification of unilateral action on the part of the Soviet Union to rectify the Berlin situation. Such action took the form of the Berlin Wall, erected on August 13, 1961. The Wall did not appear in Soviet cartoons in 1961. By 1962 it had been contorted into a protective shield to bar Western spies, fascists and agitators from entering East Berlin and East Germany. (See Cartoons VI-30, p. 98 & 31, below.)

Margaret Chase Smith, riding a broom like a witch, and Vice-President Johnson, who visited Berlin in 1961, were two of the American figures attacked in cartoons on West Berlin. (See Car-

Оккупационные власти США, Англии и Франции несут ответственность за совершаемые фашистскими бандами из Западного Берлина провокации против ГДР.   (Из газет).

Мы не несем ответственность за берлинские инциденты...

Рисунок Н. Лисогорского

VI-31

WE ARE NOT RESPONSIBLE
FOR BERLIN INCIDENTS . . .
by N. Lisogorsky

"The U.S., English, and French occupation authorities are responsible for the provocations against the German Democratic Republic committed by Fascists gangs from West Berlin."

PRAVDA, September 10, 1962, p. 3.

ВИЦЕ-ПРЕЗИДЕНТ США ДЖОНСОН: «В Западном Берлине я видел плоды демократии».
(«Нейес Дейчланд», ГДР).

VI-32 "U.S. VICE-PRESIDENT JOHNSON:
'I SAW THE FRUITS OF DEMOCRACY
IN WEST BERLIN.' "

—From Neues Deutschland (East Berlin)
IZVESTIA, August 25, 1961, p. 1.

toon VI-32, above.) Great Britain and France were also held responsible, together with the United States and West Germany, for failure to resolve the Berlin question. Substantially the same accusations were made throughout 1962: West Berlin was a spy nursery, and an aggressive NATO outpost; it provided encouragement for West Germna fascists, spies, and provocateurs. Cartoons emphasized the special liability of the three Western powers for any incidents that might erupt in Berlin. West Berlin Mayor Willy Brandt elicited especially bitter barrages. The attacks on Berlin remained substantially unchanged for the seven years from 1958 to 1964, but the numbers of cartoons in 1963 and 1964 were smaller than in the previous two years.

Cartoons on West Germany remained at about the same level through the four years. Cartoons in 1961, as in previous years, portrayed West Germany as the successor to Hitler's Third Reich.

ЛИЦО БОННСКИХ РЕВАНШИСТОВ.   Рис. М. Абрамова.

VI-33

THE FACE OF THE BONN AVENGERS
by M. Abramov

"We don't want repetition, we don't want some sort of new Hitler with another name—for example, with the name of Adenauer, Brandt or Strauss—to unleash war anew and again to commit misdeeds more barbaric than those which the Fascists committed against our people."

—From the reply of N. S. Khrushchev to questions from C. Sulzberger of The New York Times.

Hitler's face is composed of the names "Adenauer," "Brandt," and "Strauss."

PRAVDA, September 11, 1961, p. 5.

VI-34

THE BLIND MAN AND HIS GUIDE
by B. Efimov

"One must come to the conclusion that Bonn's blind policy, carried on for many years, is unfortunately continuing."

—From a speech of N. S. Khrushchev

The dog is labeled: "Revenger"; Erhard's cane: "Hallstein Doctrine."

IZVESTIA, June 17, 1964, p. 1—color.

СЛЕПОЙ И ЕГО ПОВОДЫРЬ.   Рис. Бор Ефимова

Khrushchev's statement that a new Hitler was being created in the combination of Adenauer, Brandt, and Strauss inspired a cartoon combining the three names into a portrait of Hitler. (See Cartoon VI-33, below) Adenauer, holding United States rockets, cast a shadow not of himself, but of Hitler (*Pravda,* September 1, 1961). Adenauer's warmongering was attributed to the whispered advice of Hitler's and Dulles' ghosts (*Pravda,* August 13, 1961). West German generals formulated military plans around a swastika-shaped table (*Pravda,* April 9, 1961). West German domination over military bases in England and Scandinavia was asserted (*Pravda,* March 9 and November 14, 1961).

ФРАНКО-БОННСКИЙ СОЮЗ

ЕГО ВЕРШИНА...

...И ОСНОВАНИЕ
Рис. Бор. Ефимова

VI-36

THE FRANCO-BONN ALLIANCE
by B. Efimov

"Its Top . . . and Its Base."

IZVESTIA, January 25, 1963, p. 1.

ПАУКИ В БАНКЕ.   Рисунок Кукрыниксы.

VI-35   SPIDERS IN THE JAR
by Kukryniksy

West Germany strangles France, which is kicking England. The jar is labeled "The Common Market."

PRAVDA, February 3, 1963, p. 5.

In 1962 Adenauer continued to be related to Hitler. On July 12, in a *Pravda* cartoon, he bragged that he had surpassed Hitler. This was based on Khrushchev's observation that Hitler's military budget from 1933 to 1939 was 90 billion marks, while Adenauer's from 1950 to 1961 was 100 billion. *Izvestia* on June 8, 1962, showed Defense Minister Strauss receiving an honorary diploma from the United States for his armament race, while Hitler's ghost in academic robe hovered behind. West Germany trampled over French and British bases, and the United States supplied atomic weapons to the retaliatory figures of Strauss and Adenauer (*Izvestia,* July 20, 1962). In June, 1964, Erhard appeared in color, wearing swastika

blinders, leading Germany along the road to re-
taliation. (See Cartoon VI-34, p. 100.)

Perhaps because of the Soviet Union's own
problems in the socialist camp, in 1963 and 1964
its cartoons gave special emphasis to the divisions
and conflicts of interest which separated the Western allies. Cartoons emphasized West German influence not only in military, but in economic and
political affairs of Europe. The difficulties within
the Common Market pointed to Germany as the
ultimate victor in the struggle between Great Britain and France. In "Spiders in the Jar" the West
German spider kills de Gaulle, who has already
killed the British spider. The cover of the jar is
a silver dollar. (See Cartoon VI-35, p. 101.) A
similar cartoon, also by Kukryniksy, had appeared
ten years earlier; the United States spider killed
the West European spider in a jar labeled "Organization for European Economic Cooperation."
(See Cartoon V-2, p. 42.) Another cartoon depicted how West Germany watched while both
France and the United States competed for its
favor (*Izvestia,* July 4, 1963). Despite superficial
appearances of equality, West Germany dominated
France ("The Franco-Bonn Alliance—Its Top and
Its Base"). (See Cartoon VI-36, p. 101.) Adenauer's retirement marked no change in warmongering
policy. Revenge was the burden Adenauer trans-
ferred to his successor. (See Cartoon VI-37, left.)

ЧИТАЯ РЕЧЬ Н. С. ХРУЩЕВА

Такой кусок в горло не пролезет...

Передача груза от «канцлера ухо-
дящего»...

Простой американец: →
Чему же верить?
Рисунки Бор. Ефимова.

Сердца трех.

VI-37

**READING THE SPEECH
BY N. S. KHRUSHCHEV**
by B. Efimov

"Such a bite can't be swallowed."
The small "NATO" dog drools for the large frontier
signpost labeled "German Democratic Republic."
"Freight transfer from the 'departing Chancellor.'"
Adenauer unloads a box with a soldier labeled
"Revenge."
"The average American: 'Which should I believe?'"
He holds the peaceful speech by President Kennedy
at American University, and a militant speech by the
U.S. President a few days later in West Berlin.
"Three Hearts."
France and the United States are both wooing West
Germany.

IZVESTIA, July 4, 1963, p. 4.

VI-38

ON THE PREVIOUS COURSE
by B. Efimov

"Unchanged are certain Western personages who, having hardly recovered from the shock caused by the Caribbean crisis, have again begun to sing the 'Cold War.'"

—N. S. Khrushchev

The pirate flag is labeled "Policy of Force," and the boat crew is drinking a toast "To the Cold War."

IZVESTIA, January 3, 1963, p. 2.

На Западе не перевелись такие деятели, которые, едва оправившись от потрясения, вызванного карибским кризисом, стали вновь воспевать «холодную войну»...
Н. С. ХРУЩЕВ.

Прежним курсом...
Рис. Бор. Ефимова.

СЛУШАЯ РЕЧЬ Н. С. ХРУЩЕВА

«Право», о котором мечтают «горячие головы»...

Место жандармскому мундиру — на свалке ..

Пора снять с глаз повязку!
Рис. В. Фомичева.

VI-39 LISTENING TO THE SPEECH OF N. S. KHRUSHCHEV
by V. Fomichev

" 'The law,' that 'hot heads' dream about. . . ." The book labeled: "The U.N. Constitution;" the boot: "Aggression."
"The place for the police coat—on the scarecrow. . . ." The police coat is labeled: "World policeman."
"It is high time to take off the blindfold!"

IZVESTIA, August 29, 1964, p. 2.

НЕ ТЕ СИЛЫ У КАПИТАЛИЗМА, НЕ ТА ТЯГА! (Из доклада товарища Н. С. Хрущева о Программе Коммунистической партии Советского Союза на XXII съезде КПСС).

Рис. Бор. ЕФИМОВА.

VI-40

"THERE IS NO SUCH STRENGTH IN CAPITALISM, NO SUCH PULLING POWER."

—From the report of Comrade N. S. Khrushchev to the Twenty-Second Party Congress.

by B. Efimov

The wheels of the train are marked "NATO, SEATO, and CENTO." The engine is labeled "Armaments Race." The smoke reads: "ANTI-COMMUNISM."

IZVESTIA, November 6, 1961, p. 6.

VI-41

PRAVDA'S FIFTIETH ANNIVERSARY
by Kukryniksy

The sign on the lightning bolt (in the form of a pen) reads "Pravda." The other
three signs from left to right read: "Menshevik," "Interventionists," and "Lie."

PRAVDA, May 5 ,1962, p. 6.

WESTERN CAPITALISM, IMPERIALISM, AND COLONIALISM

The numbers of cartoons in these categories were small at all times. Khrushchev's statements to the Twenty-Second Party Congress inspired many cartoons, most of which prophesied the approaching doom of capitalism and the triumph of socialism. The hypocrisy of "humanitarian capitalism" inspired many cartoon contrasts with the strength and vitality of communism. The ideological message of the Twenty-Second Party Congress with regard to the negative aspects of capitalism and imperialism was woven around Khrushchev's pronouncements, as were many other cartoons based on his remarks. (See Cartoons VI-38, 39, p. 103 and 40, p. 104.) Such impersonal themes specified no country but sustained the general level of propaganda. Cartoons on more specific topics had Belgium, Portugal, and Spain in the focus of attention, the first two countries because of their colonial policies and Spain

Зловещая тень НАТО над Кипром...
Рис. Ю. Кершина.

VI-43   NATO'S OMINOUS SHADOW
OVER CYPRUS
by IU. Kershin

IZVESTIA, February 1, 1964, p. 1.

ЧОМБОМЕТАТЕЛЬ   Рис. М. Абрамова.

VI-42   TSHOMBE-BOMB
by M. Abramov

PRAVDA, September 7, 1964, p. 3.

because of its fascist taint. Cartoons frequently depicted the United States, France, and West Germany competing for Franco's attention. Greece and Turkey, South Korea and South Vietnam (and especially Ngo Dinh Diem) appeared as ruthless dictatorships under United States direction.

Both the 40th anniversary cartoon honoring *Krokodil* (*Izvestia,* August 26, 1962) and the cartoon celebrating the 50th anniversary of *Pravda* praised the monumental achievements of those two publications over the years of fighting imperialist intrigues and the forces of reaction. (See Cartoon VI-41, p. 105.)

Colonialism and neo-colonialism were generally infrequent topics of Soviet domestic cartoons. Two basic types of cartoons appeared on these topics: the colonialist in decay, and the hidden dangers of neo-colonialism. (See Cartoons VI-42, 43, this page & 44, p. 107.) A cartoon of the first type showed determined Asian people preventing

the British lion from sowing the seeds of conflict
(September, 1963). Cartoons on the Peace Corps,
representing the other type, emphasized the potential dangers of that body disguised by the slogan
"peace" (*Izvestia,* April 25, 1961). *Pravda* reminded its readers again of the sinister purpose of
the Peace Corps in its New Year's Eve cartoon
(December 31, 1963).

In cartoons on colonialism the peoples of those
countries suppressed by colonialist policies have
all the healthy and positive attributes normally
ascribed to Soviet citizens. Asian, African, and
Latin American masses, like the Russians, vigor-
ously combat the forces of reaction.

CARTOONS PRAISING THE SOVIET UNION

This type of cartoon did not appear as
frequently in early years of the Cold War. After
Soviet space accomplishments and particularly in
connection with the Twenty-Second Party Congress

VI-44   DESIRES OF AN OLD ROBBER
by B. Efimov

"Military preparations by the Western Powers against
the People's Republic of Zanzibar and Pemba create
a dangerous situation in that area."
The British lion is gazing greedily on islands labeled
"Zanzibar" and "Pemba."

IZVESTIA, January 28, 1964, p. 1.

VI-45   WELCOME TO OUR DEAR GUEST, KHRUSHCHEV!
by N. Dolgorukov

"Today the motorship 'Armenia' is arriving at the Egyptian port of Alexandria.
'Welcome' say the people of the United Arab Republic to their important guest,
N. S. Khrushchev, a messenger of peace and friendship."

PRAVDA, May 9, 1964, p. 1.

Плакат художника Ираклия Тоидзе.

VI-46

PROGRAM OF THE COMMUNIST

PARTY OF THE SOVIET UNION
by I. Toidze

Work
Peace
Freedom
Equality
Happiness

PRAVDA, September 4, 1961, p. 1.

МЕЖПЛАНЕТНОЕ ИНТЕРВЬЮ

— А скажите, дорогая, чем объясняются ваши успехи?
— Начальными буквами слов, находящихся на мне: Советская власть, Социализм, Свобода, Равенство.   Рис. И. Семенова.

VI-47   INTERPLANETARY INTERVIEW
by I. Semenov

Planets ask the earth: "Tell me, dear, how do you explain your successes?"
The earth, marked USSR: "With the letters that you see on me, which stand for:
Soviet rule, Socialism, Freedom, and Equality." (In Russian the initial letters spell U.S.S.R.)

PRAVDA, August 12, 1962, p. 5.

in 1961, cartoons praising the Soviet Union were a significant proportion of the annual output of cartoons, especially in *Pravda*. During 1961, between August and December, a large number of cartoons were devoted to the Twenty-Second Party Congress. These cartoons applauded the successes of Soviet society and the leadership of its Communist vanguard. Emphasis on ideological content, especially in cartoons appearing around the time of the Congress, was a characteristic of 1961. Besides praising the Soviet Union, some cartoons at the same time criticized the West; but the criticisms were in terms of the evils of Western

capitalism, rather than in terms of specific countries, policies, or individuals. In 1962, space accomplishments of the Soviet Union received the largest number of accolades. In 1963 Castro became a prominent feature and many cartoons jointly praised the Cuban leader and his Soviet comrades. In 1964 Khrushchev's friendly visits abroad to Egypt and the Scandinavian countries were hailed with cartoon cheers. (See Cartoon VI-45, p. 107.) His abrupt and humiliating dismissal would eliminate one friendly image from the Soviet cartoon.

The much-heralded Program of the CPSU, and

especially its slogan "For Work, Peace, Freedom, Happiness, and Equality," was the subject of all types of visual propaganda—*plakaty* (posters) and cartoons. (See Cartoon VI-46, p. 109.) *Izvestia* used the slogan to contrast, in a black-and-white cartoon (October 17, 1961), the friendly comradely relationship among men in the Socialist camp with the wolf-like spirit in the Western jungle. Another paired cartoon in *Izvestia* (August 4, 1961) contrasted work, peace, freedom, happiness, and equality in Soviet society and their absence in the West. Efimov, in a series of five cartoons, parodied "peace" in the United States as the armaments race and fascist aggression, "work" as unemployment, "freedom" as the imprisonment of the Statue of Liberty, "equality" as the reign of the Ku Klux Klan, and "happiness" as the right of the capitalist pig to devour gold from its trough. The "Review of 1961" cartoons on December 31, 1961, in *Izvestia* glorified the achievements of the CPSU and the tasks set by the new Party program and contrasted them with the disastrous events of the capitalist West in 1961: miscarriage of the Cuban invasion; the loss of Portuguese Goa; failure of Tshombe and his colonialist masters; the reign of the Ku Klux Klan. The Soviet budget and economic plan for 1962, designed to promote peace and to benefit all mankind, counseled the general superiority of the Soviet system over the Western systems designed for aggression and exploitation *(Izvestia,* December 12, 1961).

The successful launching of Vostoks III and IV for two and three-day trips orbiting the earth in August, 1962, was the subject of several cartoons glorifying the achievements of the Soviet Union not only in space but also as the most progressive nation in all other respects. One showed the planets around the sun interpreting the meaning of "USSR" as "Soviet system, Socialism, Freedom, and Equality." (See Cartoon VI-47, p. 109.) Other cartoons showed United States dizziness at Soviet space successes or jealousy at Soviet superiority. Presidents Truman and Eisenhower, the Pentagon, and Adenauer, were shown crying "It's always East! East! Where is the

West?" (See Cartoon VI-48, below.) The *Izvestia* cartoon of August 26, appearing with the article "Dollar Cosmos" ridiculed the American Apollo moon project and declared lunar military bases a lunatic notion.

In 1963 *Pravda* cartoons in January and February glorified the mighty U.S.S.R. and the Soviet military tradition; those in early April routed for the trip to the moon. The end of April and early May welcomed Fidel Castro and praised the bond of brotherhood joining the Soviet and Cuban peoples. December repeated the slogans of the Twenty-Second Party Congress and glorified Lenin as the leader in the march for Communist

КОСМИЧЕСКИЙ КОМПАС

— Что же это делается, господа? Все «Восток» да «Восток»... А где же Запад?!!
Рисунок В. ЕФИМОВА.

VI-48

COSMIC COMPASS
by B. Efimov

"What are we to do, gentlemen? It is always 'East' and 'East'. . . . And where is the West??!"
The four points of the compass are marked: "East 1, 2, 3, and 4," in reference to the Soviet satellites.

IZVESTIA, August 19, 1962, p. 5.

victory. *Izvestia's* cartoons glorifying the Soviet Union were fewer and they appeared in June honoring Vostoks V and VI and in August praising the signing of the limited nuclear test ban treaty.

A review of cartoons over the four years shows that the level of attack diminished somewhat in 1963 and 1964 from the levels attained in 1960. However, the numbers and sharpness of Soviet cartoons in the sixties remained well above what it had been in the fifties.

Following Khrushchev's dismissal as Premier, both papers continued the usual anti-American and anti-Western propaganda through their cartoons. All the major *Pravda* and *Izvestia* cartoonists praised the feats of the Soviet cosmonauts. In the realm of international politics Soviet cartoonists continued to attack the preparations of the United States and West Germany to sign a nuclear force agreement, the pro-Nazi policy of West Germany, United States meddling in the South Vietnamese crisis, and American support for Tshombe and the Bolivian dictatorship. Other cartoons cheered the coming showdown between France and Germany in the Common Market agricultural dispute, Southern Rhodesia was condemned for suppressing Negroes, the joint naval and amphibious maneuvers of the United States and Spain were protested, and Adenauer was featured as a vulture screeching: "I want revenge; I need atomic weapons."

The cartoons immediately after the Khrushchev era were the mixture as before—a reaffirmation of the cartoon propaganda onslaught against the West despite the "peaceful coexistence" tune played by the new Kremlin leadership.

Comparing the approaches of the two major Soviet newspapers, one finds a somewhat broader horizon and greater versatility in *Izvestia* cartoons on the United States in the appearance of such themes as the Peace Corps. *Pravda* held more repetitiously to the topics of racial discrimination, absence of political freedom, capitalist exploitation of American workers, and the identity of the two political parties in the United States. *Pravda* comments were more ideological, while the *Izvestia* approach was more pragmatic, responding to events as they occurred.

Despite some innovation in technique and content, the cartoon retained its place as a weapon of persuasion in the Cold War. The cartoon remained in the same club with other methods of communication that rely on "that extraordinary and new international jargon based on recapitulation and recombination of some sixty or seventy phrases with which we are familiar, and which has so thoroughly debased a number of the most common and necessary words of political discourse."[6]

PART THREE

SOVIET PROPAGANDA POLICIES
IN THE COLD WAR

Soviet foreign policy and foreign propaganda efforts continue to be linked to the objective of fostering and accelerating world-wide social revolution.

FREDERICK C. BARGHOORN
(Soviet Foreign Propaganda, Princeton, 1964).

CHAPTER SEVEN

THE NEW LOOK

IN SOVIET CARTOONS

What are we to make of this Soviet press? The question is crucial to the whole discussion of the "democratization" of Soviet society, for there can hardly be a trend toward more democratic practices without an informed public.

Certainly Khrushchev's press is a great improvement over Stalin's. Just as certainly, it is not a free press. All of the controls and all of the dictation from above remain. The difference is in how the controls are applied—in the length of the leash.

LEO GRULIOW[1]

A new look in the Soviet press emerged slowly and cautiously following Stalin's death in March, 1953. By July, 1955, the time of the Geneva Summit Conference, the technical make-up of *Pravda* and *Izvestia* had changed. No longer was the front page dull and monotonous, full of telegrams and greetings to Stalin and only rare pictures to offset the grayness of the repetitious slogans: "Glory to Stalin," "Pledges to Stalin," "Show Us the Right Way, Stalin."

Immediately preceding the foreign ministers' talks in Geneva of May, 1959, renewed signs of change were evident. An article on Siberia, by *The New York Times* correspondent Max Frankel, appeared in early May in *Izvestia*. On May 9, 1959, *Pravda* published almost the full text of President Eisenhower's Gettysburg speech on foreign policy.

Upon his assumption of the editorship of *Izvestia* in June, 1959, Aleksei Adzhubei continued to implement the changes in make-up and content that he introduced earlier as the editor of *Kom-*

somol'skaia Pravda, making *Izvestia* a much livelier and more sophisticated paper. On November 20, 1959, both Moscow newspapers printed the text of Secretary of State Herter's conciliatory speech on foreign policy. *Izvestia* in the same month also presented Mrs. Roosevelt's views on the international situation. The Vienna meeting of Kennedy and Khrushchev on June 4–5, 1961, was the occasion for the printing in both papers of the text of a speech by President Kennedy and his picture.

These changes were more evident in *Pravda* and *Izvestia* than in other Soviet newspapers. *Izvestia* was more experimental than *Pravda* in some respects, the most notable being Adzhubei's interview with President Kennedy in the fall of 1961. Harrison Salisbury has commented on the response to this innovation:

This interview was an experiment in unshackling Russian minds, in permitting Soviet citizens to read a reasoned statement of the American position. I found Russians pouring over the Kennedy text in deep Siberia and even in Outer Mongolia. I watched them read it on the day of publication, standing in the wind and snow before the street bulletin boards for fifteen or twenty minutes, absorbing every word of a full page of type.[2]

. . . I conceded that the regime was trying bold innovations. . . . Adzhubei was a controversial figure in Soviet Society. There were not a few important men who made no secret of their dislike for him. They criticized his flashy innovations in *Izvestia* and said he had committed a disservice to his country by trying to interview and argue with President Kennedy at the same time, doing rather badly at both . . .

Adzhubei seemed to follow a double-gaited line. *Izvestia* was open to both liberal viewpoints and the neo-Stalinists. His associates, however, were among the most hard-nosed of the neo-Stalinists. Semichastny and Pavlov actively preached violence against nonconformists. They had no qualms about riding roughshod over the new legal reforms. It was this group which backed the use of the death penalty to terrorize collective farmers who didn't look after their machinery and bookkeepers who cooked the government accounts. They stirred up campaigns against the churches, inveighed against the private garden plots and personal automobiles, denounced abstract painters as parasites and terrorized innocent young couples who danced in Western-style cafes. If power fell in the hands of these ambitious men of no principle there would be trouble ahead for Russian men of good will.[3]

However, *Izvestia* did not report in detail Adzhubei's second visit and talks with President Kennedy on January 30–31, 1962.

Other changes were also evident at this time, not all of them limited to the press. Llewelyn Thompson, then American Ambassador in Moscow, appeared on television, and there were proposals for a Kennedy-Khrushchev television exchange. In the press, there was an increase of stories reprinted from the Western non-communist press, some of them not representing solely the Soviet viewpoint. An article by James Wechsler, editor of the *New York Post*, that appeared in

that paper on September 22, 1961, was reprinted in full by *Pravda* (September 26) and *Izvestia* (September 27). Wechsler's article praised President Kennedy and at one point severely criticized Premier Khrushchev. The presentation of the article in both papers, despite its content, which was at odds with the usual Soviet view, marked a milestone in Soviet newspaper coverage.

On the other hand, the use made of Walter Lippmann's columns in the Soviet press was more typical. In May of 1960, at the time of the Paris Summit Conference, the Soviet papers printed several of Walter Lippmann's columns that were severely critical of American foreign policy. However, in some of the columns reprinted, Lippmann's comments critical of the Soviet Union were deleted; and, of course, when Lippmann focused his entire column on the Soviet Union, with biting criticism, these columns did not appear.

How did the new look affect Soviet cartoons? Since 1959, *Izvestia* has been the more militantly anti-Western paper in its cartoons and in every year (1959–1964) surpassed *Pravda* in both total number of foreign affairs cartoons and in the number and percentage of those with anti-American content (See Appendix IV). In contrast to *Pravda,* it showed no diminishing of cartoon comment before the Paris talks in 1960. Yet, at the same time, it has been *Izvestia* that has been the most open to innovations, particularly in its news reporting and feature stories. This to some extent confirms the differentiated behavior in the two papers. While *Pravda* cartoons were generally less imaginative, *Izvestia* cartoons were more sophisticated and they commented in larger numbers upon foreign developments, as had been specified in the directives of the Central Committee of the CPSU, noted above. However, preeminence of *Pravda* in the field of domestic topics was not firmly established. In 1960 and 1961, *Izvestia* led *Pravda* in cartoons on domestic issues, while Pravda led in 1962. But in 1961 *Pravda* took the leading role in discussing the Twenty-Second Party Congress and its implications (an ideological, rather than a domestic topic), and

Khrushchev's attack upon abstract art, for example, was reflected in December, 1962, in four *Pravda* cartoons and only in one *Izvestia* cartoon. From 1960 through 1962, *Pravda* had more cartoons by far praising the Soviet Union (including prominently the Communist Party and Premier Khrushchev), while *Izvestia* had fewer in this category and more dealing with external enemies.

Despite the minor differences between *Pravda* and *Izvestia* (and it must be emphasized that the differences were minor), certain tendencies in the treatment of cartoons were evident in all Soviet papers and all cartoons. There were three main types of Soviet cartoons employed in comment on international happenings: the *karikatura,* the conventional type of Soviet cartoon, directed

against external enemies, the West and the United States; those contrasting in an unfavorable light the West with the Soviet Union or colonial peoples (the black-and-white contrast cartoon); and those in which the Soviet Union was, without exception, portrayed in favorable hues and tones. Another category, as yet not fully developed, concerns relations among the socialist countries.

ANTI-AMERICAN AND ANTI-WESTERN CARTOONS

There was a tendency to depict Western and especially American political leaders such as Presidents Truman, Eisenhower, and Kennedy; Vice-Presidents Nixon and Johnson; Secretaries of

МОЛЧАНИЕ СОТЧАЯНЬЯ...

Американские реакционеры, и в том числе экс-президент Трумэн, истерически призывают встретить приезд Н. С. Хрущева «заговором молчания». Для осуществления этой идеи м-р Трумэн может:

Набрать в рот воды [преимущественно мутной]. Рисунок Бор. Ефимова.

Запереть челюсти на замок.

Можно прибегнуть и к помощи дратвы.

Помогает также и основательно забитая пробка.

Впрочем, м-ру Трумэну и ему подобным нечего беспокоиться: им так или иначе придется «прикусить язык»...

VII-1   THE SILENCE OF DESPAIR
by B. Efimov

"*American reactionaries, including ex-President Truman, hysterically appeal for a 'conspiracy of silence' to meet N. S. Khrushchev's journey. To achieve this idea Mr. Truman can:*
    Pour water (preferably muddy) into his mouth,
    Lock his jaws,
    And possibly resort to the aid of heavy thread.
    A firmly driven cork would also help.
    However Mr. Truman and those like him are alarmed in vain. One way or another they will have to 'bite their tongues.'"

The last box contains clouds marked "World response to Khrushchev's journey." Truman is eating his tongue labeled "conspiracy of silence." The cartoon refers to Khrushchev's second trip to the United States, after the U-2 incident.

PRAVDA, September 16, 1960, p. 5.

State Acheson, Dulles, Herter, and Rusk; along with specific business and military figures, as symbols of cold war treachery. President Eisenhower was shown, for example, as a sinister figure with hairy arms holding in one hand his speech delivered during Captive Nations Week and in the other a set of jail keys reading "freedom." The jail, with dollar signs for its window bars, held Latin American and Southeast Asian countries enslaved by the United States. Truman became a standard feature in Soviet cartoons only when he was no longer President. (See Cartoon VII-1, p. 117.) Eisenhower was featured only after the U-2 episode (although he had appeared before becoming President). Kennedy appeared occasionally, more often in reprints of Western cartoons than in the works of Soviet cartoonists. When Kennedy appeared in Soviet cartoons, frequently his face was not shown. For example, when *Izvestia* depicted Kennedy greeting the ransomed Bay of Pigs prisoners (January 6, 1963), only his back was shown. President Johnson was depicted only once as Vice-President, in August, 1961, and not at all as President. In 1958, as Senator, he was attacked for his zealous activities on behalf of the outer space program.

A second group characterized the United States (in the person of Uncle Sam or a prototype military leader from the Pentagon or a businessman) as the symbol of deceit, aggression, and exploitation. It was always the United States that was portrayed as the leader of the aggressive NATO alliance, the United States that dominated its allies and bore responsibility for the arms race and for the tensions that threatened peace and security.

A third group consisted of those cartoons aimed at the West as a whole. In the late forties and early fifties, attention was focused on Great Britain and Churchill who, with the United States, bore the main brunt of criticism as the warmongers of the West. As Britain's relative power declined and that of Germany increased, cartoons shifted to West German militarism, especially after West Germany's entrance into NATO. And as de Gaulle

VII-2 SONG OF YESTERDAY
by Kukryniksy

"International public opinion ridicules the attempts by Washington and Tokyo to justify the failure of their unpopular policy by awkward references to 'Communist intrigue.'"
The sign says "Music by the Pentagon, Lyrics by Hitler." The tuba is playing the tune "International Communism is To Blame for Everything."

PRAVDA, June 19, 1960, p. 5.

consolidated his power in France and became a force on the international scene, he likewise became a target of cartoon ire: for flirting with West Germany, and for his refusal to sign the limited nuclear test ban treaty. Throughout the entire period there was an increasing focus on the United States with West Germany in the background—an amalgamation which could only raise the Soviet people's fears of the United States. The entire Western defense system of military alliances was depicted as fascist military schemes, with emphasis on the roles of Spain, West Germany, Japan, Korea, and the German generals Speidel and Heusinger. (See Cartoon VII-2, p. 118.

The fourth group, primarily anti-German cartoons, relied heavily upon Nazi symbols to heighten the cartoons' impact upon the Russian mind. Hitler-like images were applied to the West German government. Such cartoons were not merely anti-German; by inference they extended the sphere of German influence by pointing to Bonn's influence upon the policies of other NATO countries.

Both papers, but especially *Izvestia,* placed increased reliance on cartoons taken from foreign papers. Critical comments were taken not only from satellite and communist publications, but also from the non-communist Western press, such as *The Washington Post* and the *New York Herald Tribune,* as well as from eminent British, French, and West German papers.

THE CARTOON OF CONTRAST

Here the cartoonist portrayed the Soviet Union in a favorable light and the West, by striking contrast, in an unfavorable light all within the same cartoon. The half of the cartoon pertaining to the Soviet Union was usually light, showing sunshine behind, with clean strokes presenting a robust Soviet worker or healthy, strong people; the half of the cartoon devoted to the West was usually dark, with more cluttered lines presenting Western figures on a much smaller scale, weak, deformed, repulsive, and sinister. The over-all image was one of Soviet superiority over a Western world predestined to failure.

The simple black-and-white technique was used by Soviet cartoonists to separate the peace-loving Soviet Union and the struggling colonial peoples from the imperialist aggressors and oppressors.

(See Cartoon VII-3, below.) A classic example was the cartoon "Open Skies According to Americans—A Wave of Provocation and Espionage; Open Skies According to the Soviet Union—The Path For the Progress of Science." Praises of the Soviet system and its advantages over the Western system, particularly in space accomplishments, showed the Soviet worker on a scale five times that of the small trembling capitalist, as in "I Accuse" and "Learn, Gentlemen." (See Cartoon VII-4, p. 120.)

Когда наооды рвут цепи...

...Этих спускают с цепи!..

Рисунок Н. Лисогорского.

VII-3

"WHEN PEOPLE BREAK THEIR (COLONIAL) CHAINS, (UNCLE SAM) UNCHAINS THESE DOGS: AGGRESSION, PROVOCATIONS, AND SLANDER."
by N. Lisogorsky

The liberated peoples break chains which are dollar signs or spell out "colonialism."

PRAVDA, July 23, 1960, p. 1.

CARTOONS GLORIFYING THE SOVIET UNION

Glorification of Soviet accomplishments had as the main topics Soviet successes in space, (See Cartoon VII-5, right) Premier Khrushchev and the Communist Party as leaders in the struggle for peace, and the strength and power of Soviet society as revealed through the strong, healthy Soviet workers. Many of the cartoons praising the Soviet Union (and other types of cartoons as well) were inspired in theme by statements of Premier Khrushchev.

An important innovation in Soviet cartoons was the introduction of Soviet leaders into positive political cartoon. Premier Khrushchev first appeared in *Pravda* on January 1, 1960. On March 18, 1960, *Izvestia* drew him leaving for Paris as a symbol of friendship, sincerity, and

VII-4

I ACCUSE!
by N. Lisogorsky

The figure of "peace" points its finger at Powers and his accomplices.

PRAVDA, August 20, 1960, p. 5.

С ДНЕМ РОЖДЕНИЯ!

Празднование дня рождения дедушки Бип-Бип 1-го.
Рис В. Фомичева.

VII-5   **"HAPPY BIRTHDAY!"**
"CELEBRATION OF THE BIRTHDAY
OF GRANDFATHER BEEP-BEEP THE FIRST."
by V. Fomichev

Future cosmic rockets, other sputniks, school children, and the space dogs Belka and Strelka congratulate the first sputnik on his birthday.

IZVESTIA, October 3, 1960, p. 3.

peace. Although the cult of personality was officially declared taboo, pictures and cartoons of Khrushchev appeared more frequently than had those of Stalin, thus confirming, in part, the charges leveled against Khrushchev. (See Cartoon VII-6, p. 121.) As a consequence of the denunciation of the cult of personality, Soviet cartoonists for some time to come may be reluctant to use statements of Soviet leaders as the inspiration for their cartoons.

A different aspect of the new look was the appearance, in 1959, of cartoons favorable toward the United States, in the booklet *Vo Imia Mira*.

The presence of even two such cartoons was unusual and the experiment was not repeated until August 8, 1963, when *Izvestia* printed a cartoon showing just the hands of the United States, Great Britain, and the Soviet Union signing the nuclear test ban treaty. The Kremlin propagandists did not again depict friendly faces of their Western adversaries.

RELATIONS WITHIN THE SOCIALIST CAMP

The cartoon was employed extensively in the Soviet campaign against the Yugoslav Communist Party, and particularly against its leader, Marshal

VII-7

TOWARDS WHAT DOES THE HEAD
OF REVISIONISM WORK?
by M. Abramov

The wall is labeled "Solidarity of the Socialist Countries."

PRAVDA, May 7, 1958, p. 4.

VII-6

THE POWERFUL VOICE OF MILLIONS
by N. Dolgorukov

Premier Khrushchev is the powerful voice of millions, who in various languages demand "peace," "disarmament," a condemnation of "espionage flights," and "freedom for dependent and colonial countries."

IZVESTIA, September 30, 1960, p. 2.

Tito. The most vile epithets were hurled against the Yugoslavs and against those implicated in the Titoist heresy, the Hungarian Laszlo Rajk and the Bulgarian Traicho Kostov. In recent years, however, Soviet treatment through cartoons of relations within the Communist bloc has been more cautious. *Pravda,* on May 7, 1958, carried a cartoon showing "Revisionism" attacking in vain the strong wall of "Solidarity of the Socialist Countries." (See Cartoon VII-7, below.) This was a rather vague reference, in contrast to the specific accusations of the early 1950's.

In regard to the Soviet anti-Stalin campaign, it is the *absence* of cartoons that is revealing.

Khrushchev's denunciation of Stalin's excesses and of the cult of personality were not recorded in any cartoons in *Pravda* or *Izvestia*. Scanning cartoons in other Soviet publications uncovered only one cartoon directly attacking the cult of personality, or Stalin. It appeared in *Krokodil* of December 10, 1962. This cartoon was in two parts; the first showed an older Party functionary fervently giving his support to the "resolutions and decisions of the Twentieth Congress of the CPSU," and the second part showed him at home kneeling before the lower two-thirds of a portrait unmistakably of Stalin, asking forgiveness for his behavior at the Congress.

A similar reticence to comment in cartoons in the two leading papers was observable in connec-

tion with the relations between the Communist Parties of the Soviet Union and those of Albania and China. This continued even after several years of direct and indirect attacks presented in other communications. Cartoons were gradually turned

БАГАЖ БОННСКОГО РЕВАНШИСТА.

Рисунок Кукрыниксы.

VII-9

BAGGAGE OF BONN'S REVENGER
by Kukryniksy

A West German soldier's cry for "revenge" is echoed by Hitler.

PRAVDA, May 9, 1964, p. 4.

Рис. Бор. Ефимова.

По их «образу и подобию»

VII-8   IN THEIR "IMAGE"
                      by B. Efimov

Marshal Tito grasps an axe labeled "fascist terror." He salutes portraits of Hitler, Mussolini and Himmler.

PRAVDA, August 23, 1949, p. 4.

to this topic. Such cartoon comments as were published did not appear in the two major papers but in other publications with lesser circulation. For instance a cartoon by Kukryniksy appeared in *Krokodil* (December 20, 1962). It placed Enver Hoxha, who was clearly identified, with the Pentagon and a Wehrmacht general, and all three together pulled the chariot of War. Two cartoons attacking the Chinese appeared in September, 1963. The first appeared in *Krokodil* (September 10) and criticized the Chinese for

ПРОЕКТ ПАМЯТНИКА «БЕШЕНЫМ». Рисунок Кукрыниксы.

VII-10

DESIGN FOR A MONUMENT
TO "MADMEN"
by Kukryniksy

PRAVDA, March 1, 1964, p. 5.

the Sino-Soviet dispute was reaching a stage where visual aids could be applied to reinforce the party position. There was a certain parallel with the Yugoslav-Soviet dispute of 1948. Despite the open rupture in June, 1948, anti-Tito cartoons appeared in *Pravda* and *Izvestia* and other Soviet papers and magazines only more than a year later, in the fall of 1949. However, once the attack started, it assumed very large proportions and continued with intensity for the next four years. This has not yet happened in the Sino-Soviet dispute, although the first tentative moves were

Женевский «раунд Кеннеди». Судья на ринге.
Рис. Бор. Ефимова.

VII-11

THE REFEREE IN THE RING FOR
THE "KENNEDY ROUND" AT GENEVA
by B. Efimov

The contestants in the ring are Britain, the United States, and the European Common Market.

IZVESTIA, May 6, 1964, p. 2.

their refusal to sign the nuclear test ban treaty. The title was "The Duet of the Gallic Rooster and the Peking Duck." The second appeared in *Sovetskaia Rossia* also in September. It ridiculed Chinese dogmatism and inflexibility in wanting "all or nothing." In April, 1964, a cartoon appearing in *Sovetskaia Rossia* depicted the Peking duck as a dogmatist. It is interesting that these last two cartoons appeared in a paper which is circulated only within the Russian Republic.

Perhaps the Soviet Union wished by these cartoons to answer the Chinese cartoon attacks which first appeared in January, 1962, when Chinese allegorical cartoons attacked Khrushchev under the title "Ancient Tales in Modern Form" in *Jen-mih Jih-Pao*.[4] Or it might have been that

made in including the cartoon as a weapon in the propaganda battle. It is significant that cartoons were used sparingly in pursuing Khrushchev's policy toward Mao Tse-tung and the Chinese Communist Party.

OTHER CHANGES

The Soviet cartoon still retained in 1964 some of its basic characteristics of flagrant falsification present in 1947. "In Their 'Image'," which showed Marshall Tito in August, 1949, as a fascist servant and worshiper of Hitler, Mussolini, and Himmler (See Cartoon VII-8, p. 122), is quite similar in style to the cartoons "Baggage of Bonn's Revenger" and "Design for a Monument to 'Madmen'" that appeared in *Pravda* in 1964. (See Cartoons VII-9, p. 122 & 10, p. 123.) In these cases the cartoon is based upon either absolute falsification or sheer invention by the cartoonist. Cartoons toward the end of the period surveyed were more often based on real events. The front page cartoon "Welcome!" in *Pravda* on May 9, 1964, or the cartoon of March 5, 1964, ridiculing the bullet-proof vest that Secretary of Defense Robert McNamara wore on his Saigon visit, had their genesis in fact. (See Cartoon VI-20, p. 92.) Two *Izvestia* cartoons, May 6 and 8, 1964, "Geneva 'Kennedy Round'" and "American 'Radio Day' in Athens" were also inspired by specific news events; the events were then subjected to the proper ideological interpretation by the cartoonist. (See Cartoons VII-11, p. 123 & 12, right.)

Another obvious change was the prominent display of cartoons, especially evident in *Izvestia*. Cartoons often formed an integral part of an article, or a comment to illustrate short TASS dispatches from abroad (See Cartoon VII-13, p. 125), or as a part of the front-page foreign news index, as in "Broad Hospitality in Narrow Passage" appearing in *Izvestia* March 11, 1964. (See Cartoon VI-10, p. 85.) These examples, and the fact that in 1964 *Izvestia* had 113 front-page cartoons, indicate the recent prominence given cartoons in foreign news presentation. The color picture and color cartoon introduced in *Izvestia* in the June 14, 1964, issue gave additional prominence to the cartoon and pointed to the importance ascribed this communication technique.

The new look in the Soviet press had contained

Министр греческого правительства А. Папандреу выставил за дверь чиновника американского пропагандистского агентства Джойса, который в грубой и оскорбительной форме протестовал против ограничения радиопередач «Голоса Америки».   (Из газет).

Американский «День радио» в Афинах.
Рис. Бор. Е Ф И М О В а.

VII-12

AMERICAN "RADIO DAY" IN ATHENS
by B. Efimov

"Greek cabinet minister A. Papandreou expelled from his office Mr. Joyce, an official of the American propaganda agency, who roughly and rudely protested against limitation of the radio broadcasts of the 'Voice of America.'"

Mr. Joyce holds a petition entitled "About Radio Broadcasts of the 'Voice of America.'"

IZVESTIA, May 8, 1964, p. 2.

possibilities for improving communications between East and West by presenting both points of view. This possibility, however, was not visible in the cartoon medium. Cartoons, on the contrary, emphasized the irrevocable division, the irreconcilable difference between the United States and the Soviet Union. The cartoon sector of the

ТЕЛЕГРАММЫ КОММЕНТИРУЕТ ХУДОЖНИК

РВУТСЯ КОМАНДОВАТЬ

БОНН, 12 марта. (По телеф. от соб. корр). Министр обороны ФРГ фон Хассель в беседе с группой норвежских и датских журналистов, вновь публично заявил, что Западная Германия «должна иметь большее влияние внутри НАТО», поскольку бундесвер является самой сильной армией в Европе среди членов НАТО. В настоящее время в различных штабах НАТО занято 1.530 служащих бундесвера, 30 боннских генералов занимают командные посты.

ОПАСНЫЕ «УТКИ»

АФИНЫ, 12 марта. (ТАСС). Министр иностранных дел Греции Костопулос дал распоряжение вести систематическое наблюдение за передачами «Голоса Америки» с плавучей радиостанции «Курьер», находящейся у острова Родос. Эти передачи вызвали негодование жителей острова из-за содержащихся в них антигреческих высказываний.

Рисунки В. Фомичева.

СОЮЗ ПРОТИВ АФРИКАНЦЕВ

ЛОНДОН, 12 марта. (ТАСС). Правительство Южно-Африканской Республики намерено закупить в Англии 24 военно-транспортных самолета типа «Авро-748». Игнорируя резолюцию ООН, Англия продолжает поставлять расистам ЮАР вооружение и боеприпасы. Недавно стало известно о поставке английскими фирмами шести вертолетов типа «Уосп» и о намерении ЮАР закупить в Англии подводные лодки «Оберон».

VII-13

COMMENTS OF THE ARTIST ON NEWS CABLES
by V. Fomichev

The first cartoon, about the NATO horse, depicts the increasing role of German officers in the NATO high command.
The center cartoon concerns Greek official dissatisfaction about Voice of America broadcasts from a U.S. radio ship stationed near Rhodes.
The third cartoon criticizes Britain for selling military transport planes and helicopters to South Africa, thus strengthening the latter's racist government.

IZVESTIA, March 13, 1964, p. 1.

Soviet propaganda machine, regardless of any subtle changes taking place in it, remained a long-playing broken record which endlessly reiterated the theme that the western imperialists plot the destruction of the Soviet Union; and that to this end they have erected, with the aid of fascist governments and former fascist oligarchs, a string of military alliances designed for aggression against the Soviet Union. Such practices presented to the Soviet reader an image of an unavoidable conflict.

The evolution of the cartoon over several years demonstrated, as did the more readable stories and livelier make-up, that both Soviet papers, and particularly *Izvestia,* were in the process of change. However, despite the hopeful signs that appeared in news coverage, despite the increased use of foreign cartoons in Soviet papers, despite the emergence of the positive cartoon glorifying Soviet leaders and Soviet successes, of the cartoon of contrasts, and color cartoons, there was neither a visible crack in the monolithic image presented nor a flow of diverse ideas and issues from the expanded variety of techniques and differences in style.

CHAPTER EIGHT

THE CARTOON AND

SOVIET FOREIGN POLICY,

1947-1964

The Russians do not seem to have realized that this distrust is dangerous in itself. They have been remarkably indifferent to their reputation for duplicity. The breaking of the test moratorium in the autumn of 1961 followed the formal assurance of the Soviet Government on August 28, 1959, that the Soviet Union would resume testing only if the Western Powers did so. The covert dispatch of nuclear missiles to Cuba was accompanied by public and private denials of any such intention. What commitment, then, can the Soviet Union be trusted to observe?

One lesson of Cuba was that though two nuclear Powers will shrink from nuclear war as a calculated act of policy, nuclear war could break out by accident—that is to say, by misunderstanding. The most pressing obligation on the nuclear Powers, therefore, is to remove the possible causes of misunderstanding. Probably the most potent cause of misunderstanding is the conviction that Moscow may not mean what it says and might even intend the opposite. Mr. Khrushchev ought to ponder the possible consequence of duplicity as it has been practiced in Soviet diplomacy in recent years. This kind of diplomacy ought to be discarded.

From a *Manchester Guardian Weekly* editorial
on the Soviet resumption of nuclear tests.[1]

We have now come through the forest of Soviet cartoons gathered from a seventeen year period. We have become acquainted with their objectives and their patterns through the shifts and changes in Soviet foreign policy. We may now consider the nature of the relation between the cartoons viewed and Soviet policy in this period, especially foreign policy, to see if the cartoon provides additional insight into that policy.

The propaganda and information media are closely linked to the organs of policy making and execution. The entire information process in the Soviet Union is subservient to policy objectives. The cartoon is part of a highly planned, centralized and coordinated information policy. Numerous examples confirm this role of the cartoon. The immediate cessation of anti-American cartoons after Khrushchev's speech on offensive weapons and missiles in Cuba and the immediate cartoon comment following Khrushchev's condemnation of modern art in 1962 are but two examples that illustrate this relationship.

This study has decisively illustrated the persistent Soviet representation of the West and the United States as a dangerous and provocative enemy against which the Russian nation must be prepared to defend itself. This aggressive and treacherous anti-Western image was the single most conspicuous feature of *Pravda* and *Izvestia* cartoons. Interestingly, cartoons played a special role in presenting this negative image. On several occasions the cartoon presentation of international events did not parallel the news and picture (information) or editorial (opinion) coverage of those same happenings. The cartoon made no comment on those few occasions when other Soviet news techniques demonstrated a conciliatory attitude toward the West. Even when news stories and editorials gave tentative approval of Western peaceful intentions, for example at the time of the Geneva talks in 1955, cartoons remained silent. The contrast with picture coverage was particularly noteworthy. Although Western leaders and statesmen were rarely featured in Soviet news photographs, such pictures usually appeared at times of relative relaxation of international tensions. The contrast between the cartoon and the photographic images of Presidents Truman, Eisenhower, Kennedy, and Johnson, and other Western leaders, is stark. The significance of the few photos of Western leaders is that they provided the sole source of relief from the visual images perpetuated by cartoons of the sinister war monsters who direct Western policies. The hesitation on the part of Soviet information policy to alter the images in the minds of the captive Soviet audience indicates either reluctance or fear, or both, to break down the carefully constructed image of the West.

Certain changes occurred in the function and use of the cartoon over a period of years, representing an increased reliance on visual propaganda. Following specific Party decrees in 1958 dividing the tasks of *Pravda* and *Izvestia* and statements by leading Party ideologues emphasizing the necessity of increasing the level and pace of ideological warfare, the number of cartoons increased. The decrees directed *Izvestia* to focus its attention on international developments and *Izvestia* drastically expanded its cartoon presentation of such developments. However, the use of large numbers of cartoons may have other implications as well. Because the cartoon was used in the past in connection with specific intense propaganda campaigns (the anti-Tito and anti-American campaign of June 1949–June 1950, for example), the large numbers in recent years might also have significance beyond a simple increase in numbers.

The cartoon consistently presented an ominous and belligerent image of the West. It did so in increasing numbers in later years. The hostile image was relieved only occasionally by the absence of cartoons and only once by favorable comment. The apparent objective of cartoons was to implant, repeat, and reinforce a negative image of the West in the minds of the readers.

The possible motives for such a policy appear to be twofold. First, the increased use of visual propaganda serves to fill the void created by reduction in reliance on terror in the Soviet Union. Second, the Soviet authorities might desire to maintain in the Soviet population a high level of anxiety about the West. The image of a hostile West illustrates to a population which is yearning for consumer goods why the economy must continue to bear enormous expenditures for national defense. The use of external scapegoats to distract from domestic difficulties is a common device.

The study also revealed a systematic discrepancy between the content of Soviet domestic propaganda and its proclamations abroad. While Soviet propaganda for foreign audiences was equally anti-Western, anti-imperialist, it placed greater emphasis upon the possibilities of cooperation and peaceful coexistence, confirmed with assurances of Soviet peaceful intent. Domestic propaganda in its thousands of cartoons rarely mentioned peaceful possibilities and only once noted cooperation.

Such differences in content are scarcely accidental. Both foreign and domestic propaganda are branches of the Soviet centrally coordinated information policy. Each serves as an official expression and interpretation of Soviet foreign policy developments. It can only mean that Soviet policy makers pursued a dual objective. Messages stressing coexistence and cooperation and the sincerity of Soviet peaceful intentions are part of a strategy aimed at causing the West to relax its defenses against Soviet political, military, economic, and ideological pressures throughout the world. Further, by identifying itself with a universally valued symbol—peace—the Soviet Union woos those throughout the world who wish to avoid perception of political realities, whether new nations or well-intentioned groups within older nations, and lulls them into a sense of security.

The apparent contradictions in Soviet propaganda content, whether between domestic and foreign, or in the various techniques of domestic propaganda itself, might cause us to retreat without exploring in detail the relation between Soviet cartoons and Soviet policy. Yet despite these internal contradictions, the cartoon graphically and economically illustrates Soviet presentation of explanations and interpretations of specific events to its population. Although the content of the cartoon is repetitious, simple, and obviously distorted, it contains not only an exoteric, or general, message but also an esoteric, or implied, message. Observation of cartoons can at times, within a context of all possible sources of information, provide insight into certain aspects of Soviet foreign policy. The sudden halts of cartoons in the 1948 Berlin blockade, the 1950 Korean War, and the 1962 Cuban missile confrontation, and the limited use of cartoons in the 1956 Suez-Hungarian and the 1961 Cuban "Bay of Pigs" crisis might mean that the Soviet Union was playing its own game of brinkmanship. Having reached the brink, the Soviet Union did not desire to increase the possibility of direct conflict between the United States and itself. Consistent with this policy the Soviet Union did not prepare the Soviet population for such a confrontation through the extensive use of antagonistic cartoons after the crisis emerged. Instead, such comment ceased.

On the other hand, failure to diminish antagonistic cartoons in certain situations regarded as thaw-like, such as Khrushchev's 1959 visits to the United States or the preparations for the Paris Summit Conference, might have indicated (reinforcing other observations by Soviet specialists) that the Soviet Union had no intention of concluding successful negotiations at those times despite its participation in talks. In certain cases, analysis of Soviet cartoons and other press output might have aided in making predictions. The absence of cartoons on the subject of nuclear tests in 1961 is a notable example.

Deliberate distortion of events and issues further exemplified the cartoons' portrayal of Soviet foreign policy. The cartoon was used both as a strategic and a tactical weapon. The long range strategy of the cartoon was to present an unfavorable image of the West. Short range tactics in response to changing circumstances required certain departures from the simple negative image.

The complete cartoon silence about nuclear testing for a year prior to Soviet unilateral resumption of tests in the fall of 1961 illustrates such tactical maneuvering. This topic was neglected, perhaps to avoid creating embarrassment or confusion of images in the minds of Soviet readers. Even for the unsubtle Soviet propaganda, to rant continuously against nuclear tests under those circumstances was to invite ridicule and charges of hypocrisy. However, when the Americans resumed nuclear tests, cartoons denounced American testing and blamed the West for intensifying the arms race and poisoning the atmosphere.

Treatment of the war in Vietnam exemplified an application of strategy. There was a steady increase in cartoons on this topic in 1963 and 1964 attacking American intervention and meddling, particularly the machinations of McNamara's Pentagon. The objectives are multiple. By throwing blame on the West, cartoons help to cover up the role of other foreign governments involved in the conflict. Such strategy provides a continuing means of arousing anti-American sentiment in a more immediate and apt fashion than through historic or distant involvements. Finally, such an interpretation ties the United States with imperialists and neo-colonialists against the new emerging nations of Africa and Asia.

Occasionally other tactics than emphasis were necessary, especially silence or distortions. Not all Soviet foreign policy engagements found expression in cartoons. Soviet rapprochements with the United States were ignored in cartoons as were sudden reversals in the Soviet stand and retreats from attained positions (as in the Cuban confrontation in 1962). Distortion was also a prominent feature of Soviet cartoons. Cartoons distorted events by repetitiously pounding a single theme inaccurately. Portrayal of United Nations Secretary-General Hammarskjold illustrated precisely the half-truths and outright distortions of Soviet cartoons.

Propaganda twisted and turned torturously to the oscillations of Soviet foreign policy. Whatever was required in the interest of that policy was relentlessly and repetitiously, crudely and bluntly, stamped across the printed page. No movement was arbitrary; each was subordinate to a higher objective. Through the varied phases of the Cold War, Soviet cartoons never lagged in projecting a starkly unattractive image of its opponents, real or imagined. While the Soviet Union concentrated most of its foreign propaganda on the themes of cooperation and peaceful coexistence, with the important proviso that the latter include support of anti-colonialist wars of national liberation, the cartoons of its domestic propaganda stressed the contrast and conflict between East and West. The West has been presented as a dangerous and provocative enemy. The increased use of cartoons extolling the Soviet Union, the repeated portrayal of the potential opponent in strictly unfavorable terms, the emphasis on the theme that the nation must be prepared to defend itself against aggressive forces, and the assertion of the weakness and likelihood of early defeat of the opponent if a defensive war should prove necessary—all these are elements of Soviet cartoons in the Cold War. One voice speaks to the world at large, another to the citizens at home.

Similar behavior by totalitarian and government-controlled press and other propaganda organs has in times past served to induce subject populations to approve, and not merely to tolerate, such policies as the government held necessary to protect the national interest. Propaganda of this type can contribute to the psychological preparation of the population for participation in war and even incline public opinion to favor a military solution.

This is not to say that the behavior of the Soviet press has been designed to rouse popular support and enthusiasm for a general, total war. The Soviet Union most likely has a genuine desire to avoid total nuclear war since it recognizes the destruction that would ensue. But neither has its propaganda in the form of cartoons nurtured its domestic audience to anticipate a lessening of tensions. This defensive stance harbors an element of offense within itself. The alleged necessity for preparedness against Western aggression is, at least in part, created by the Soviet Union itself. This mentality may lead to a vicious circle; for if one acts inimically, the chances are that the intended opponent will react in the same fashion. Through the cartoon medium the Soviet Union has pursued a dichotomic world view as old as the regime itself. While the supporting slogans vary from "capitalist encirclement" to "peaceful coexistence," the basic thesis of the unceasing nature of the struggle of two social systems remains unaltered. Khrushchev unmistakably reaffirmed its global character: "Coexistence is the continuation of the struggle of the two social systems . . . . We consider that it is an economic, political, and ideological struggle, but not a military one. It will be a competition of the two systems on a world scale."[2]

What the most recent power shifts in the Kremlin signify is not yet certain. But Soviet domestic propaganda of both the Stalin and the Khrushchev eras confirmed that while political leaders may come and go, may be praised while in office and damned after their downfall, the basic propaganda techniques remain substantially unaltered; that while the new wielders of power may replace the editors of *Pravda* and *Izvestia*, the technicians beneath them remain unchanged. The "cult of personality" is castigated, but those who make the critique merely readjust to a new line, still distinguished by its monotonous, repetitious, and hostile content.

If the study of cartoons shows nothing else, it shows both the Soviet flexibility in adapting to different conditions and the immutability of basic objectives. The cartoon is but a single device for communicating the objectives of the leadership, for advancing the cause of the Soviet Union. The political situation, and with it the strategy and tactics, may change. The fundamental goals of communist policy do not.

NOTES

CHAPTER ONE

1. From the Soviet Political Dictionary, cited by Donald Dunham, *Kremlin Target: U.S.A.—Conquest by Propaganda* (New York: Ives Washburn, Inc., 1961), pp. 13–14.

2. More attention has been paid to Soviet presentation of their domestic problems. There have been two presentations in English of Soviet cartoons, both based on those appearing in *Krokodil*, the Soviet humor magazine; *Krokodil* is not, however, primarily engaged in setting the official party line in foreign affairs. See William Nelson, *Out of the Crocodile's Mouth* (Washington, D.C.: Public Affairs Press, 1949). Mr. Nelson's book deals with the period 1946–1949. See also Rodger Swearingen, *What's So Funny Comrade?* (New York: Frederick A. Praeger, 1961), which covers the period 1958–1961.

3. Marshall D. Shulman, *Stalin's Foreign Policy Reappraised* (Cambridge: Harvard University Press, 1963).

4. Merle Fainsod, *How Russia is Ruled* (Cambridge: Harvard University Press, 1963), p. 580.

5. Fainsod, *op. cit.*, p. 580.

6. Shulman, *op. cit.*, p. 262.

CHAPTER TWO

1. V. I. Lenin, *Selected Works* (New York: International Publishers, 1938), Vol. X, p. 204.

2. J. V. Stalin, *Stenographic Account of the XII Party Congress, 1923,* p. 123. Cited by Marshall D. Shulman in "The Administration of the Soviet Press" (unpublished Master's Essay, Department of Government, Columbia University, December, 1948).

3. Quoted in E. L. Khudiakov, *Voprosy Zhurnalistiki* (Moskva: Izdatel'stvo Moskovskogo Universiteta, 1959), p. 263.

4. For a detailed discussion of the Soviet press, see Shulman, "The Administration of the Soviet Press," *op. cit.*, and Nikolai G. Bogdanov and Boris A. Viazemskii, *Spravochnik Zhurnalista,* (Leningrad: Lenizdat, 1961).

5. John N. Hazard, *The Soviet System of Government* (Chicago: University of Chicago Press, 1960), pp. 54–56.

6. See Appendices I and II for a summary listing of Soviet newspapers and magazines.

7. *Editor and Publisher, International Yearbook,* 1963.

8. In the decree of the Central Committee of June 6, 1958, entitled "About Improving Interpretation in the Press and Radio Coverage of Life in Socialist Countries" *Pravda* and the journals *Kommunist, Partiinaia Zhizn', Voprosy Istorii KPSS, Agitator, V Pomoshch' Politicheskomy Samoobrazovaniiu, Voprosy Filosofii,* and *Voprosy Ekonomiki* were asked to concentrate on "theoretical, political and economic themes" and ideological and party issues, while *Izvestia* was to deal with government activities and "the development of socialist democracy, presenting its superiority over bourgeois democracy." (See *Sovetskaia Pechat' V Dokumentakh* [Moskva: Gosudarstvennoe Izdatel'stvo Politicheskoi Literatury, 1961], pp. 292–293.)

The decree of the Central Committee of June 24, 1959, entitled "On the Performance of the Newspaper *Izvestia*" cited four major tasks: (1) to report about the work of the Supreme Soviet and the Government; (2) to clarify economic questions and life in the country; (3) to clarify ideological, scientific, and cultural developments; and (4) to report about international life and the foreign policy of the Soviet Union. In regard to the last, "the newspaper must constantly propagandize the foreign policy measures of the Soviet Government, the struggle of the

USSR for peace and the reduction of international tension, reveal and expose the imperialist character of foreign policies of capitalist governments and in the first place that of the USA. Another important duty of the newspaper consists of propagating in a convincing manner the idea of peaceful coexistence of states with different social-economic systems, the struggle of the USSR for the prevention of a new war, and the solution of international disputes through negotiations, revealing the plans of the capitalistic countries directed against the USSR, countries of people's democracies, and peoples struggling for liberation from colonialism. Also, one of the basic tasks is presentation of life in the countries of the socialist camp, their successes in economic, political, and cultural fields." (*Ibid.*, pp. 121–122.)

9. *Sovetskaia Pechat'*, No. 6, 1961, p. 44.

10. *Izvestia* has been an evening paper since June 1, 1960.

11. Shulman, "The Administration of the Soviet Press," *op. cit.*

12. *Ibid.*, p. 54.

13. *Ibid.*, p. 57. For a recent collection of party decrees on the question of the press, including statements by Khrushchev, see *Sovetskaia Pechat' v Dokumentakh* (Moskva: Gosudarstvennoe Izdatel'stvo Politicheskoi Literatury, 1961).

14. Shulman, "The Administration of the Soviet Press," *op. cit.*, p. 70.

15. *Ibid.*, p. 74.

16. Bogdanov and Viazemskii, *Spravochnik Zhurnalista, op. cit.*

This publication was apparently watched for and well received in the Soviet Union. It was given a long review in *Sovetskaia Pechat':* "We have long awaited such a book. . . . Yes, finally there is an entire book on the history of the Soviet Press, on the newspaper genre, the techniques of proofs, the development of poligraphy . . . the principles of the Soviet press . . ." (*Sovetskaia Pechat'*, No. 11, 1961, pp. 43–45.)

17. Bogdanov and Viazemskii, *op. cit.*, pp. 46–47.

18. *Ibid.*, p. 47.

19. *Ibid.*, p. 205.

20. *Ibid.*

21. *Ibid.*

22. *Ibid.*, p. 215.

23. *Sovetskaia Pechat' v Dokumentakh, op. cit.*, p. 478.

24. Bogdanov and Viazemskii, *op. cit.*, p. 215.

25. *Ibid.*, p. 216.

26. N. G. Pal'gunov, *Osnovy Informatsii v Gazete: TASS i Ego Rol'* (Moskva: Izdatel'stvo Moskovskogo Universiteta, 1955), p. 3.

This shows no change from the earlier statement by K. Kuzmichev in *Voprosy Zhurnalistiki* in the thirties: "All dissertations on 'objective and complete' information are liberal hypocrisy. The aim of information does not consist in commercializing news, but educating the great masses of workers, in organizing them under the exclusive direction of the party for clearly defined tasks. This aim will not be attained by objective reports of events. Liberty, objectivity of the press, these are fictions. Information is a means of class struggle, not a mirror to reflect events objectively." (Quoted in Whitman Bassow, "*Izvestia* Looks Inside U.S.A.," *Public Opinion Quarterly*, Vol. XII, No. 3, 1948.)

27. *Sovetskaia Pechat' v Dokumentakh, op. cit.*, p. 477.

28. Alex Inkeles, *Public Opinion in the Soviet Union* (Cambridge: Harvard University Press, 1950), p. 160.

Lev Nikolaevich Tolkunov, a professor of journalism, provided Soviet convictions about the conduct of Soviet and Western presses in reporting the international developments: "Imperialist propaganda does not have the vigor to oppose the victorious ideology of socialism with any life-giving fresh ideas or original conceptions. Hence the most significant meaning is ascribed to slander and misinformation, in which base lies, untrue portrayal of life in the socialist countries, and perversions of Marxist-Leninist ideas are given. Because of these exposed lies and slanders of the imperialists, first-degree attention must be paid to the wide propagation in a comprehensible manner. That activity of the press is one of the more crucial tasks that it must fulfill." (*Pechat' Evropeiskikh Stran Narodnoi Demokratii* [Moskva: Izdatel'stvo VPSH i AON pri TsK KPSS, 1959], p. 4.)

Similar views of the American press have been expressed by V. A. Cheprakov in "SShA

Segodnia: Pora Somnenii i Razdumii," *Kommunist,* No. 10, 1961, and V. IAdov, "Priemy i Metody Imperialisticheskoi Propagandy," *Kommunist,* No. 2, 1962.

29. See Theodore E. Kruglak, *The Two Faces of TASS* (Minneapolis: University of Minnesota Press, 1962).

30. Agenstvo Pechati Novosti, established in 1960, replaced the Soviet Information Bureau, whose primary function was dissemination of Soviet national news for consumption abroad. Like TASS, APN has correspondents abroad and fulfills two major tasks: it distributes Soviet domestic news to publishing media abroad, and it reports through the comments and articles of its correspondents (and less through direct news bulletins) about foreign developments for use in Soviet newspapers. There are four sponsors of APN: The Union of Journalists of the U.S.S.R.; The Union of Writers of the U.S.S.R.; the Soviet Society for Cultural Relations with Foreign Countries; and the All-Union Society for the Dissemination of Political and Scientific Knowledge. (See *Sovetskaia Pechat',* No. 7, 1961, pp. 28–29; No. 3, 1961, pp. 49–52.)

31. M. S. Cherepakov, ed., *Zhanry Sovetskoi Gazety* (Moskva: Izdatel'stvo Moskovskogo Universiteta, 1959), p. 25.

32. *Ibid.,* p. 33.

33. *Ibid.,* p. 87.

34. *Ibid.,* p. 229.

35. Bogdanov and Viazemskii, *op. cit.,* pp. 260–261.

36. *Bol'shaia Sovetskaia Entsiklopediia* (2nd ed., 1957), Vol. XX, p. 201.

37. Bogdanov and Viazemakii, *op. cit.,* p. 233.

38. Alexander Werth, *Russia Under Khrushchev* (New York: Hill and Wang, 1962), p. 229.

39. L. F. Il'ichev, "Moshchnyi Faktor Stroitel'stva Kommunizma," *Kommunist,* No. 1, 1962. Il'ichev in November, 1962, became chairman of the Ideological Commission of the Central Committee of the CPSU.

CHAPTER THREE

1. Bogdanov and Viazemskii, *op. cit.,* p. 284.

2. Boris Efimov, *Politicheskie Karikatury 1924–1934* (Moskva: Sovetskii Pisatel', 1935), p. 10.

3. Quoted in Nataliia Sokolova, *Kukryniksy* (Moskva: Izdatel'stvo Akademii Khudozhestv SSSR, 1962), p. 14.

4. Bogdanov and Viazemskii, *op. cit.,* p. 284.

5. In 1961, *Pravda* had only four cartoons on domestic topics and 174 on international affairs (including praise of the Soviet role in international affairs, Soviet scientific and other achievements). In 1962, *Pravda* had thirty cartoons on local topics and 166 on non-local topics. Fourteen of the local topic cartoons appeared in November and December and many were inspired by Khrushchev's statements on modern art. In 1961, *Izvestia* had ten cartoons on domestic issues and 216 on national and international themes. In 1962, it had fourteen on domestic and local issues and 208 on other topics.

6. Bognaov and Viazemskii, *op. cit.,* p. 296.

7. Boris Efimov, "Blizkoe Daleko," *Sovetskaia Pechat',* No. 5, May, 1962, p. 37.

8. Pavel A. Satiukov, "Sovetskie Zhurnalisty—Ispitanye Pomoschniki Kommunisticheskoi Partii," *Sovetskaia Pechat',* No. 12, December, 1959, p. 25.

9. *Ibid.*

10. Sokolova, *op. cit.,* p. 378.

11. *Izvestia,* April 14, 1962, p. 2.

12. Bogdanov and Viazemskii, *op. cit.,* p. 285.

13. *Bol'shaia Sovetskaia Entsiklopediia* (2nd ed., 1957), Vol. XX, p. 202.

14. A trio of artists whose names together form Kukryniksy: Mikhail *Ku*prianov, Profirii *Kry*lov, and *Ni*kolai Sokolov.

15. Abram Terz (pseudonym), *The Trial Begins* (New York: Pantheon Books, Inc., 1960), p. 85.

16. For example, Benjamin Franklin's famous cartoon, "Join, or Die," which unified the American colonists on the eve of the American Revolution.

17. *The Guns of August* (New York: Macmillan, 1962), p. 313.

18. Jacob Burck, quoted in Gayle A. Waldrop, *Editor and Editorial Writer* (New York: Rinehart and Co., 1955), p. 457.

19. Harry Ladd Smith, quoted in Waldrop, *op. cit.,* p. 458.

Herblock's caricature of Vice President Nixon (*The Washington Post,* January 2, 1960, p. 8) which depicted him as a witch surrounded by all the tools of witchcraft, and Cummings' cartoon (*The Daily Express,* August 17, 1959, p. 4) that pictured President de Gaulle and Chancellor Adenauer laying a wreath on the grave of Pierre Laval, both exemplify the dangers of overstatement and inaccuracy, even in the hands of two very prominent cartoonists.

20. Michael Cummings, *These Uproarious Years,* a Pictorial Post-war History (London: McGibbon and Kee, 1954), from the foreword, p. i.

CHAPTER FOUR

1. Sacha Simon, "A Correspondent in Moscow," *Problems of Communism,* Vol. XII, No. 1 (January-February, 1963), pp. 41–42.
2. Alexander Dallin, "America Through Soviet Eyes," *Public Opinion Quarterly,* Vol. XI, No. 1, 1947.
3. Whitman Bassow, "*Izvestia* Looks Inside U.S.A.," *Public Opinion Quarterly,* Vol. XII, No. 3, 1948, p. 439.
4. Frederick C. Barghoorn, *The Soviet Image of the United States, A Study in Distortion* (New York: Harcourt, Brace and Co., 1950), p. 126.

CHAPTER FIVE

1. *How Russia Is Ruled, op. cit.,* p. 341.
2. Editorials from the two papers were examined, and several in *Pravda* made reference to the West's interest in working for peace. Of the 14 editorials dealing with international affairs that appeared in *Pravda* between January and July of 1955, the first three, appearing between January 19 and February 14, were anti-United States in tone; the following four, between February 20 and April 10, were anti-Western. On April 16, "Austrian Peace Treaty—Work of All" admitted that there had been good will on both sides; but on April 27, *Pravda* followed with an anti-Western editorial and on May 10, with one directed against the French and British. The May 16 editorial was mildly critical of the West, while on May 22, the editorial commented favorably about both East and West. June 9, showed a mild anti-West German editorial; and on June 15, a rather neutral one, "For Lessening of International Tension, For Strengthening of Trust Among Countries," was presented.

3. The number of cartoons on domestic events in *Pravda* increased in 1956 to twenty-four while in the other years surveyed (1947–1955) it was usually two or three; the main topic was bureaucracy, probably as a result of the emphasis on that issue at the Twentieth Party Congress. *Izvestia* had only three cartoons on domestic problems.

4. The Khrushchev visit showed once again the difficulties encountered by the Soviet Union in understanding the United States. Whether by accident or design, this habitual misunderstanding bodes ill for Soviet-American relations. Supporting evidence for this view is the fact that Soviet Ambassador Anatoly Dobrynin has publicly admitted that the Soviet Embassy experts have never been able to provide completely adequate economic information and analysis. They are simply caught in an ideological straight jacket. Another amusing example of the same misconceptions was seen when Soviet radio and press commentators were thrown into confusion over the American steel companies' yielding to Presidential power and rescinding their price increases. This should not have happened, according to Soviet theory. See Tad Szulc, *The New York Times,* April 26, 1962.

5. Harrison Salisbury, *The New York Times,* May 17, 1960, p. 17. For another interpretation, see Alexander Dallin, *The Soviet Union at the United Nations* (New York: Frederick A. Praeger, 1962), especially pp. 129–34, 156, 168.

6. The U-2 incident and the Paris conference received extensive coverage in the Soviet press. *Komsomol'skaia Pravda* printed eight cartoons between May 6 and 31, while *Kazakhstanskaia Pravda* of Alma-Ata had nine. The themes were the same as those in the two major papers. In *Komsomol'skaia Pravda* they were approached in a manner more arresting to the youthful imagination (depicting the Pentagon as a gangster, for example, in "Imperialist Hybrid" and "Following the Appearance" or "American

Espionage Factory According to *Newsweek Magazine*" or "In the Clutches of the Devil"). The Sherlock Holmes approach could be seen in the story accompanying one of the cartoons, "The Affair of the Black Jet," which, like others in the paper, relied on suspense, mystery, intrigue, and the "cloak-and-dagger" motif.

7. For a detailed consideration of Soviet policy in the United Nations, see Dallin, *The Soviet Union at the United Nations, op. cit.*

CHAPTER SIX

1. "Leninskoi Pravde—50 Let," *Sovetskaia Pechat'*, No. 6, June, 1962, p. 14.

2. *Pravda,* April 16, 30, May 20, June 23, and July 10, 1962. *Izvestia,* February 18, April 25, and June 12, 1962.

3. *Pravda,* February 10 and *Izvestia,* January 31, 1962.

4. *Pravda,* January 5 and March 7, 1962.

5. The troika system refers to the Soviet Union's demand for a reorganization of the Secretariat. This plan would give the Western, Communist, and neutral blocs equal representation at all levels of the Secretariat, including the Secretary-General. The troika proposal was a logical maneuver by the Soviet Union to prevent the Secretary-General from bypassing the Security Council, thus circumventing the veto. By politicizing the office of the Secretary-General, and having a Soviet representative as one of three secretaries, the Soviet Union would introduce the same safe-guards as in the veto.

6. Donald Macrae, *Ideology and Society* (New York: The Free Press of Glencoe, Inc., 1962), p. 187.

CHAPTER SEVEN

1. Leo Gruliow, "The Role of the Press," *Problems of Communism* Vol. XII, No. 1, January-February, 1963, p. 40.

2. Harrison E. Salisbury, *A New Russia?* (New York: Harper and Row, 1962), p. 128.

3. *Ibid.,* p. 131–132.

4. Arthur A. Cohen, "Peking's Picture Puzzles," *Problems of Communism,* Vol. XI, No. 4, July-August, 1962, p. 59.

CHAPTER EIGHT

1. *Manchester Guardian Weekly,* Vol. 87, No. 26, December 27, 1962, p. 1.

2. *Pravda,* October 14, 1959.

BIBLIOGRAPHY

1. Books

ABRAMOV, M. and EFIMOV, B.: *Vo Imia Mira*, Moskva, Gospolitizdat, 1959.

BARGHOORN, FREDERICK C.: *Soviet Foreign Propaganda*, Princeton, Princeton University Press, 1964.

—— *The Soviet Image of the United States, A Study in Distortion*, New York, Harcourt, Brace and Co., 1950.

BOGDANOV, N. G. and VIAZEMSKII, B. A.: *Spravochnik Zhurnalista*, Leningrad, Lenizdat, 1961.

CHEREPAKOV, M. S. (ed.): *Zhanry Sovetskoi Gazety*, Moskva, Izdatel'stvo Moskovskogo Universiteta, 1959.

CUMMINGS, MICHAEL: *These Uproarious Years—A Pictorial Post-War History*, London, McGibbon & Kee, 1954.

DALLIN, ALEXANDER: *The Soviet Union at the United Nations*, New York, Frederick A. Praeger, 1962.

DUNHAM, DONALD: *Kremlin Target: U.S.A.—Conquest by Propaganda*, New York, Ives Washburn, Inc., 1961.

EFIMOV, BORIS: *Politicheskie Karikatury 1924–1934*, Moskva, Sovetskii Pisatel', 1935.

—— *Za Prochnyi Mir, Protiv Podzhigatelei Voiny*, Moskva, Izdatel'stvo Iskustvo, 1950.

FAINSOD, MERLE: *How Russia Is Ruled*, Cambridge, Harvard University Press, 1963.

HAZARD, JOHN N.: *The Soviet System of Government*, Chicago, University of Chicago Press, 1960.

INKELES, ALEX: *Public Opinion in the Soviet Union*, Cambridge, Harvard University Press, 1950.

JAMES, HENRY: *Daumier—Caricaturist*, London, Rodale Press, 1954.

KHUDIAKOV, E. L.: *Voprosy Zhurnalistiki*, Moskva, Izdatel'stvo Moskovskogo Universiteta, 1959.

KRUGLAK, THEODORE E.: *The Two Faces of TASS*, Minneapolis, University of Minnesota Press, 1962.

LENIN, V. I.: *Selected Works*, New York, International Publishers, 1938.

MACRAE, DONALD: *Ideology and Society*, New York, The Free Press of Glencoe, Inc., 1962.

NELSON, WILLIAM: *Out of the Crocodile's Mouth*, Washington, D.C., The Public Affairs Press, 1949.

OZMITEL', E. K.: *Sovetskaia Satira*. Moskva, Izdatel'stvo Prosveshchenie, 1964.

PAL'GUNOV, N. G.: *Osnovy Informatsii v Gazete: TASS i Ego Rol'*, Moskva, Izdatel'stvo Moskovskogo Universiteta, 1955.

SALISBURY, HARRISON E.: *A New Russia?* New York, Harper & Row, 1962.

SAMUILOV, V. S. (ed.): *Sovetskaia Pechat' v Period Mezhdu XX i XXII S"ezdami KPSS*, Moskva, Izdatel'stvo Svesoiuznoi Knizhnoi Palaty, 1961.

SHULMAN, MARSHALL D.: *Stalin's Foreign Policy Reappraised*, Cambridge, Harvard University Press, 1963.

—— "The Administration of the Soviet Press," Unpublished Master's Essay, Department of Government, Columbia University, December, 1948.

SOKOLOVA, NATALIIA: *Kukryniksy*, Moskva, Izdatel'stvo Akademii Khudozhestv SSSR, 1962.

STYKALIN, S., and KREMENSKAIA, I.: *Sovetskaia Satiricheskaia Pechat' 1917–1963*, Moskva, Gospolitizdat, 1963.

SWEARINGEN, RODGER: *What's So Funny Comrade?* New York, Frederick A. Praeger, 1961.

TERZ, ABRAM (pseudonym): *The Trial Begins*, New York, Pantheon Books, Inc., 1960.

TOLKUNOV, L. N.: *Pechat' Evropeiskikh Stran Narodnoi Demokratii*, Moskva, Izdatel'stvo VPSH i AON pri TsK KPSS, 1959.

TUCHMAN, BARBARA: *The Guns of August*, New York, Macmillan, 1962.

TUCKER, ROBERT C.: *The Soviet Political Mind*, New York, Frederick A. Praeger, 1963.

USSR: *Newspapers and Magazines of the USSR,* Moscow, Mezhdunarodnaia Kniga, 1961.

——— *Sovetskaia Pechat' V Dokumentakh,* Moskva, Gosudarstvennoe Izdatel'stvo Politicheskoi Literatury, 1961.

WALDROP, GAYLE A.: *Editor and Editorial Writer,* New York, Rinehart & Co., 1955.

WERTH, ALEXANDER: *Russia Under Khrushchev,* New York, Hill & Wang, 1962.

ZHIVEINOV, N. I.: *Kapitalisticheskaia Pressa SShA,* Moskva, Gosudarstvennoe Izdatel'stvo Politicheskoi Literatury, 1956.

2. *Articles*

BASSOW, WHITMAN: "Izvestia Looks Inside U.S.A." *Public Opinion Quarterly,* Vol. XII, No. 3, 1948.

Bol'shaia Sovetskaia Entsiklopediia, (2nd ed.) Vol. XX, 1957.

CHEPRAKOV, V. A.: "SShA Segodnia: Pora Somnenii i Razdumii," *Kommunist,* No. 1, 1962.

COHEN, ARTHUR A.: "Peking's Picture Puzzles," *Problems of Communism,* Vol. XI, No. 4, July-August 1962.

DALLIN, ALEXANDER: "America Through Soviet Eyes," *Public Opinion Quarterly,* Vol. XI, No. 1, 1947.

DAVISON, W. P.: "An Analysis of the Soviet Controlled Berlin Press," *Public Opinion Quarterly,* Vol. XI, No. 1, 1947.

Editor and Publisher International Yearbook, 1963.

EFIMOV, BORIS: "Blizkoe Daleko," *Sovetskaia Pechat',* No. 5, May 1962.

GRULIOW, LEO: "The Role of the Press," *Problems of Communism,* Vol. XII, No. 1, January-February 1963.

IADOV, V.: "Priemy i Metody Imperialisticheskoi Propagandy," *Kommunist,* No. 2, 1962.

IL'ICHEV, L. F.: "Moshchnyi Faktor Stroitel'stva Kommunizma," *Kommunist,* No. 1, 1962.

LIVELY, JAMES: "Propaganda Techniques of Civil War Cartoonists," *Public Opinion Quarterly,* Vol. VI, No. 1, 1942.

MOSELY, PHILIP E.: "How the Kremlin Keeps Ivan in Line," *The New York Times Magazine,* February 19, 1961.

SATIUKOV, PAVEL: "Leninskoi Pravde—50 Let," *Sovetskaia Pechat',* No. 6, June 1962.

——— "Sovetskie Zhurnalisty--Ispitanye Pomoshchniki Kommunisticheskoi Partii," *Sovetskaia Pechat',* No. 12, December, 1959.

SOIUZ ZHURNALISTOV SSSR: *Sovetskaia Pechat',* Nos. 2, 3, 6, 7, 11, 1961.

SIMON, SASHA: "A Correspondent in Moscow," *Problems of Cummunism,* Vol. XII, No. 1, January-February 1963.

APPENDIX I

ALL-UNION AND UNION REPUBLIC PUBLICATIONS

According to the official Soviet guide, *Newspapers and Magazines of the USSR—1961* (Moscow: Mezhdunarodnaia Kniga), all Soviet newspapers and magazines are divided into three major sections:

A. ALL-UNION AND RSFSR NEWSPAPERS

In addition to *Pravda* (365 issues) and *Izvestia* (300), the following newspapers are listed: *Vodnyi Transport* (156), *Gudok* (300), *Komsomol'skaia Pravda* (300), *Lesnaia Promyshlenost'* (156), *Literatura i Zhizn'* (156), *Literaturnaia Gazeta* (156), *Meditsinskii Rabotnik* (104), *Moscow News* (104), *Nedelia* (*Izvestia's* Sunday supplement, 52), *Les Nouvelles de Moscou* (104), *Pionerskaia Pravda* (104), *Sel'skaia Zhizn'* (300), *Sovetskaia Kul'tura* (156), *Sovetskaia Rossiia* (300), *Sovetskaia Torgovlia* (156), *Sovetskii Sport* (300), *Stroitel'naia Gazeta* (156), *Trud* (300), *Uchitel'skaia Gazeta* (156), *Ekonomicheskaia Gazeta* (300). *Za Rubezhom* (publication of the Union of Journalists of the USSR, 52), as well as *Sovetskii Flot* and *Sovetskaia Aviatsiia,* were not listed. (For more detailed information on the military periodical press see Raymond L. Garthoff, *Soviet Strategy in the Nuclear Age* [New York: Frederick A. Praeger, 1962], pp. 271–287.)

B. ALL-UNION AND RSFSR MAGAZINES

Magazines are divided into eleven categories. Only a partial listing is offered here from approximately 2,000 titles listed.

I. Economics, Sociology, Politics: *Agitator* (24 issues), *Kommunist* (18), *Krokodil* (36), *Mezhdunarodnaia Zhizn'* (published in English as *International Affairs,* 12), *Novoe Vremia* (published in English as *New Times* and also in French, German, and Spanish, 52), *Partiinaia Zhizn'* (24), *Sovetskaia Pechat'* (12), *Sovetskii Soiuz* (published in English as *Soviet Union* and in twelve other languages, [12]).

II. Scientific Journals: *Voprosy Istorii* (12), *Voprosy Istorii KPSS* (6), *Voprosy Filosofii* (12), *Voprosy Edonomiki* (12), *Istoricheskii Arhiv* (6), *Istoriia SSSR* (6), *Mirovaiia Ekonomika i Mezhdunarodnye Otnosheniia* (12).

III–VI represent: National Economy, Agriculture, Medicine, and Public Health, Art-architecture.

VII. Literary Magazines: *Druzhba Narodov* (12), *Zvezda* (12), *Znamia* (12), *Kul'tura i Zhizn'* (published in English as *Culture and Life* and also in French, Spanish, and German, [12]), *Inostrannaia Literatura* (12), *Neva* (12), *Novyi Mir* (12), *Ogonek* (52), *Sovetskaia Literatura* (also published in English as *Soviet Literature* and in German, Polish, and Spanish, [12]),

VIII. Magazines for the Young: *Veselye Kartinki* (12), *Vokrug Sveta* (12), *Molodaia Gvardiia* (12), *Pioneer* (12), *IUnost'* (12).

IX–XI deal with Physical Culture, Educational and Pedagogical Magazines, and Magazines on International Democratic Organizations.

C. NEWSPAPERS AND MAGAZINES OF THE SOVIET UNION REPUBLICS

Each of the remaining fourteen republics have two papers, one in the national language and the other in Russian, published jointly by the Central Committee of the Communist Party, the Council of Ministers, and the Supreme Soviet of the Republic. For example, the Kazakh SSSR has *Kazakhstanskaia Pravda* (in Russian, 300) and *Sotsialistik Kazakhstana* (in Kazakh, 300). The exceptions are the Ukraine, where there are two Russian-language papers (*Pravda Ukrainy, Rabochaia Gazeta*) and two in Ukrainian (*Radians'-*

ka Ukraina, Robitnycha Gazeta); the Estonian SSSR, where there are one Russian and two Estonian papers; Lithuania and the Uzbek SSSR, where there is one Russian-language paper each and one in each of the national languages, Polish and Lithuanian, and Uzbek and Tadzhik. There are a few other papers published in the republics that deal with specific groups of people or professional interests (workers, peasants, youth, etc.).

APPENDIX II

MAJOR SOVIET NEWSPAPERS AND MAGAZINES

Komsomol'skaia Pravda is the publication of the Central Committee of the Young Communist League of the Soviet Union (Komsomol). It is the third largest national paper, with a circulation of 3.4 million.[1] *Pionerskaia Pravda,* the national paper read by Pioneri (children between ten and fifteen years of age) has a circulation of three million.[2]

Among the many other professional or specialized newspapers distributed throughout the Soviet Union a few may be mentioned: *Trud,* published by the Central Committee of Trade Unions with a circulation of 1.4 million; *Krasnaia Zvezda,* published by the Ministry of Defense of the Soviet Union (circulation not listed for this or any other military newspaper, including *Sovetskii Flot* and *Sovetskaia Aviatsiia); Literaturnaia Gazeta,* published by the Union of Soviet Writers with a circulation of 850,000 and generally considered a national paper of literary interest; and *Za Rubezhom,* a weekly paper published since June 25, 1960, by the Union of Soviet Journalists with a circulation of 200,000, consisting mainly of translations from the world press heavily accenting press reports from satellite countries and those neutral nations highly critical of the West.

In addition to publishing *Pravda,* the Central Committee of the Communist Party of the Soviet Union publishes such nationally circulated newspapers as *Ekonomicheskaia Gazeta* (circulation not listed) and *Sel'skaia Zhizn'* (900,000 issues).

In addition to the papers published nationally there are newspapers jointly published by the Communist Party, Council of Ministers, and the Supreme Soviet of each Republic, *oblast',* or city. For example, *Sovetskaia Rossia,* with a circulation of two million, is printed in 10 cities of the RSFSR and is published by the Russian Republic Communist Party Bureau and the Russian Republic Council of Ministers. *Moskovskaia Pravda* is published by the Moscow Province Communist Party and Soviet and has a circulation of 500,000; and *Vechernaia Moskva* is published by the Moscow City Communist Party Bureau and Soviet and has a circulation of 225,000.

Republican newspapers — for example, the Alma-Ata *Kazakhstanskaia Pravda* — carry less international news but more republic or regional news than *Pravda* and *Izvestia.* But from time to time they reprint editorials directly from *Pravda* discussing important domestic or national affairs. For example, *Pravda's* editorial of May 18, 1960, explaining the summit failure, was reprinted without comment or identification in *Kazakhstanskaia Pravda* on May 19, 1960.) In this manner the official party interpretation receives broad circulation across the Soviet Union. Radio Moscow's editorials and news stories are available to newspapers as supplements to the dispatches sent by TASS news agency. Radio Moscow reads at dictation speed its own editorials, as well as some editorials and news features taken from *Pravda,*

---

[1]*Editor and Publisher International Yearbook,* 1963, p. 481.

[2]*Ibid.* All circulation figures, unless otherwise noted, are from the same source.

to assist newspaper editors in compiling their copy.

There are also numbers of national magazines published weekly, bi-monthly, or monthly.

Kommunist is a theoretical journal of the Central Committee of the Comunist Party of the Soviet Union. Another Party publication is *Partiinaia Zhizn'*. *Agitator* is its specialized monthly publication on propaganda and agitation. *Sovetskaia Pechat'*, a monthly by the Union of Soviet Journalists, deals with theoretical or technical aspects of newspaper publishing.

Other scientific journals, such as *Voprosy Istorii, Voprosy Edonomiki, Voprosy Filosofii,* and *Mirovaia Edonomika I Mezhdunarodnye Otnosheniia,* are but a few among many magazines published in the Soviet Union.

The theoretical journal of the International Communist movement is *Problemy Mira I Sotsialisma*[3] which in 1958 replaced the defunct *For A Lasting Peace, For A People's Democracy*. It is a general information journal of the Communist and Workers' Parties throughout the world and is published in Prague.

Other specialized magazines for national and international consumption are: *Kul'tura i Zhizn'*, an illustrated magazine carrying extensive "information about the achievements of the Soviet people in the spheres of state construction, the development of Soviet national economy, culture, and science.[4] *Sovetskaia Literatura (Soviet Literature)* published "the best new works by Soviet authors—novels, short novels, plays, short stories, sketches, and poetry. . . . Each issue has several colored reproductions of pictures by well-known painters, drawings, sculpture, and architecture."[5] *Novyi Mir, Zvezda,* and *Neva* are some of the many literary magazines published only in the Russian language. A more popular type of magazine is *Ogonek*[6], a pictorial publication in the manner of *Life* or *Look*. It is a weekly and primarily for national consumption. *Soviet Union* is a general magazine for international consumption. Other magazines are directed more to specfic areas of the world. *USSR* is distributed in United States and the United States publication *America* is available in the Soviet Union. *Afrika i Asiia Segodnia* is a monthly magazine published since 1961 by the Soviet Academy of Sciences. It contains articles supporting the Soviet Union's self-appointed role as the devoted friend and ally of those peoples who, from past and present experience, know colonial rule. The fact that the Soviet Union itself endured the hindrance of "capitalist encirclement" is an argument used to woo these emerging nations. *Krokodil*[7] is a weekly humor magazine and is very popular in the Soviet Union.

---

[3]The North American, English-language edition of *Problemy Mira i Sotsialisma* is *World Marxist Review: Problems of Peace and Socialism*. It is printed in Toronto. The journal is also published in French, Chinese, Bulgarian, Czech, Dutch, German, Hungarian, Italian, Japanese, Korean, Mongolian, Polish, Rumanian, Spanish, Swedish, and Vietnamese.

[4]*Newspapers and Magazines of the USSR, op. cit.,* p. 258.

[5]*Ibid.*

[6]Circulation 1,850,000 (*Sovetskaia Pechat'*, No. 6, 1961, p. 44).

[7]Circulation 1,500,000 (Sovetskaia Pechat', No. 6, 1961, p. 44).

APPENDIX III

Number of Cartoons Appearing in Pravda and Izvestia (2746)

PRAVDA (1191)

	1947	1948	1949	1950	1951	1952	1953	1954	1955	1956	1957	1958	1959	1960	1961	1962	1963	1964
Jan.		2	1	2	1	—	9	2	6	3	6	17	9	17	19	23	7	11
Feb.		—	—	4	2	2	5	—	5	2	2	—	4	5	13	16	10	9
Mar.		—	—	12	—	3	1	3	8	1	5	3	3	7	11	19	1	8
Apr.		—	2	4	—	3	—	1	1	1	—	2	5	4	13	16	4	2
May	1	—	3	7	—	3	—	—	3	1	3	7	11	38	3	17	7	6
June	3	—	—	3	—	2	—	1	—	—	3	—	16	29	8	15	6	13
July	—	—	7	—	—	—	—	1	—	1	3	8	6	16	9	14	2	6
Aug.	—	—	14	1	—	—	—	1	—	1	2	9	9	19	33	19	4	—
Sept.	—	—	13	—	—	—	—	1	—	1	1	3	13	17	11	3	6	5
Oct.	6	—	13	—	1	—	3	2	—	—	5	10	10	25	20	6	2	8
Nov.	—	—	3	—	2	1	7	5	—	4	3	7	14	18	18	3	10	14
Dec.	—	—	3	—	—	10	4	7	3	8	15	7	13	23	16	15	10	20
Total:	10	2	56	33	3	24	29	24	26	23	46	73	113	218	174	166	69	102

IZVESTIA (1555)

	1947	1948	1949	1950	1951	1952	1953	1954	1955	1956	1957	1958	1959	1960	1961	1962	1963	1964
Jan.		1	—	8	—	1	5	3	1	2	2	7	6	25	16	15	22	37
Feb.		—	—	6	—	—	4	1	—	—	1	—	2	13	20	18	22	27
Mar.		—	—	18	—	—	—	1	5	—	—	1	1	16	23	12	16	28
Apr.		—	—	11	1	1	—	4	4	1	1	—	1	16	16	12	4	13
May		—	1	3	1	3	1	1	2	—	—	8	7	28	17	11	16	14
June	—	—	1	—	—	2	—	2	1	—	3	4	20	26	8	18	15	18
July	1	—	1	2	—	2	—	—	—	—	—	4	20	27	32	16	13	21
Aug.	—	—	1	3	—	—	—	1	1	—	1	2	18	34	28	28	10	19
Sept.	1	—	14	—	1	—	—	1	—	—	—	—	18	25	9	25	11	20
Oct.	4	—	17	—	1	1	1	—	—	—	1	4	17	31	13	16	15	21
Nov.	2	—	17	1	2	2	1	1	—	1	2	3	15	30	15	12	31	21
Dec.	—	1	4	—	—	5	3	—	1	2	5	3	13	25	19	25	13	26
Total:	8	2	56	52	6	16	15	15	15	6	17	36	138	296	216	208	188	265

Absence of an entry indicates that the month was not surveyed. A dash indicates that there were no cartoons in the surveyed month.

APPENDIX IV

CARTOON ATTITUDES EXPRESSED BY PRAVDA AND IZVESTIA

(Figures in the left hand columns below signify the number of anti-American cartoons by month; in the center columns, anti-Western; and in the right hand columns, pro-Russian.)

1947

	Pravda		—	Izvestia		
Jan.	—	—	—	—	—	—
Feb.	—	—	—	—	—	—
Mar.	—	—	—	—	—	—
Apr.	—	—	—	—	—	—
May	—	—	—	—	—	—
June	1	—	—	—	—	—
July	3	—	—	1	—	—
Aug.	—	—	—	—	—	—
Sept.	—	—	—	1	—	—
Oct.	6	—	—	4	—	—
Nov.	—	—	—	2	—	—
Dec.	—	—	—	—	—	—
Total:	10	—	—	8	—	—
Percent	100	0	0	100	0	0

1948

	Pravda		—	Izvestia		
Jan.	2	—	—	—	1	—
Feb.	—	—	—	—	—	—
Mar.	—	—	—	—	—	—
Apr.	—	—	—	—	—	—
May	—	—	—	—	—	—
June	—	—	—	—	—	—
July	—	—	—	—	—	—
Aug.	—	—	—	—	—	—
Sept.	—	—	—	—	—	—
Oct.	—	—	—	—	—	—
Nov.	—	—	—	—	—	—
Dec.	—	—	—	—	1	—
Total:	2	—	—	—	2	—
Percent	100	0	0	0	100	0

1949

	Pravda		—	Izvestia		
Jan.	1	—	—	—	—	—
Feb.	—	—	—	—	—	—
Mar.	—	—	—	—	—	—
Apr.	2	—	—	—	—	—
May	3	—	—	1	·	—
June	—	—	—	—	1	—
July	—	—	—	1	—	—
Aug.	5	2	—	—	1	—
Sept.	8	6	—	9	5	—
Oct.	11	2	—	11	6	—
Nov.	11	2	—	14	3	—
Dec.	1	1	1	2	2	—
Total:	42	13	1	38	18	—
Percent	75	23	2	68	32	0

1950

	Pravda		—	Izvestia		
Jan.	1	1	—	5	3	—
Feb.	2	2	—	5	1	—
Mar.	10	2	—	11	7	—
Apr.	2	2	—	9	2	—
May	6	1	—	3	—	—
June	1	2	—	—	—	—
July	—	—	—	1	1	—
Aug.	—	—	—	3	—	—
Sept.	1	—	—	—	—	—
Oct.	—	—	—	—	—	—
Nov.	—	—	—	—	1	—
Dec.	—	—	—	—	—	—
Total:	23	10	—	37	15	—
Percent	69	31	0	71	29	0

1951

	Pravda			Izvestia		
Jan.	1	—	—	—	—	—
Feb.	2	—	—	—	—	—
Mar.	—	—	—	—	—	—
Apr.	—	—	—	1	—	—
May	—	—	—	1	—	—
June	—	—	—	—	—	—
July	—	—	—	—	—	—
Aug.	—	—	—	—	—	—
Sept.	—	—	—	1	—	—
Oct.	—	—	—	1	—	—
Nov.	—	—	—	2	—	—
Dec.	—	—	—	—	—	—
Total:	3	—	—	6	—	—
Percent	100	0	0	100	0	0

1952

	Pravda			Izvestia		
Jan.	—	—	—	1	—	—
Feb.	2	—	—	—	—	—
Mar.	3	—	—	—	—	—
Apr.	3	—	—	1	—	—
May	3	—	—	3	—	—
June	2	—	—	2	—	—
July	—	—	—	2	—	—
Aug.	—	—	—	—	—	—
Sept.	—	—	—	—	—	—
Oct.	—	—	—	—	—	—
Nov.	1	—	—	2	—	—
Dec.	9	1	—	5	—	—
Total:	23	1	—	16	—	—
Percent	96	4	0	100	0	0

1953

	Pravda			Izvestia		
Jan.	4	5	—	4	1	—
Feb.	2	3	—	3	1	—
Mar.	1	—	—	—	—	—
Apr.	—	—	—	—	—	—
May	—	—	—	1	—	—
June	—	—	—	—	—	—
July	—	—	—	—	—	—
Aug.	—	—	—	—	—	—
Sept.	—	—	—	—	—	—
Oct.	2	1	—	1	—	—
Nov.	7	—	—	—	1	—
Dec.	4	—	—	2	1	—
Total:	20	9	—	11	4	—
Percent	69	31	0	73	27	0

1954

	Pravda			Izvestia		
Jan.	1	1	—	2	1	—
Feb.	—	—	—	1	—	—
Mar.	2	1	—	1	—	—
Apr.	1	—	—	2	2	—
May	—	—	—	—	1	—
June	1	—	—	2	—	—
July	1	—	—	—	—	—
Aug.	1	—	—	1	—	—
Sept.	1	—	—	1	—	—
Oct.	—	2	—	—	—	—
Nov.	3	2	—	1	—	—
Dec.	2	5	—	—	—	—
Total:	13	11	—	11	4	—
Percent	54	46	0	73	27	0

1955

	Pravda			Izvestia		
Jan.	1	5	—	—	1	—
Feb.	2	3	—	—	—	—
Mar.	4	4	—	3	2	—
Apr.	1	—	—	2	2	—
May	1	2	—	1	1	—
June	—	—	—	—	1	—
July	—	—	—	—	—	—
Aug.	—	—	—	—	1	—
Sept.	—	—	—	—	—	—
Oct.	—	—	—	—	—	—
Nov.	—	—	—	—	—	—
Dec.	2	1	—	1	—	—
Total:	11	15	—	7	8	—
Percent	42	58	0	47	53	0

1956

	Pravda			Izvestia		
Jan.	1	1	1	—	2	—
Feb.	—	—	2	—	—	—
Mar.	—	1	—	—	—	—
Apr.	—	—	1	—	—	1
May	—	—	1	—	—	—
June	—	—	—	—	—	—
July	1	—	—	—	—	—
Aug.	—	1	—	—	—	—
Sept.	—	1	—	—	—	—
Oct.	—	—	—	—	—	—
Nov.	1	3	—	—	1	—
Dec.	4	3	1	1	—	1
Total:	7	10	6	1	3	2
Percent	30	44	26	17	58	33

1957

	Pravda		—	Izvestia		
Jan.	5	1	—	1	1	—
Feb.	2	—	—	1	—	—
Mar.	4	1	—	—	—	—
Apr.	—	—	—	—	—	1
May	2	1	—	—	—	—
June	3	—	—	3	—	—
July	2	—	—	1	—	—
Aug.	1	—	—	1	—	—
Sept.	3	2	—	—	—	—
Oct.	—	—	1	—	—	1
Nov.	3	—	—	1	—	1
Dec.	8	4	3	4	1	—
Total:	33	9	4	12	2	3
Percent	72	19	9	70	12	18

1958

	Pravda		—	Izvestia		
Jan.	7	9	1	5	1	1
Feb.	—	—	—	—	—	—
Mar.	—	1	2	—	1	—
Apr.	2	—	—	—	—	—
May	3	4	—	3	2	3
June	—	—	—	2	2	—
July	6	2	—	1	2	1
Aug.	7	2	—	2	—	—
Sept.	3	—	—	—	—	—
Oct.	6	2	2	3	—	1
Nov.	5	1	1	2	1	—
Dec.	5	1	1	—	2	1
Total:	44	22	7	18	11	7
Percent	60	30	10	50	31	19

1959

	Pravda		—	Izvestia		
Jan.	1	1	7	2	1	3
Feb.	1	2	1	1	1	—
Mar.	1	1	1	1	—	—
Apr.	3	2	—	—	1	—
May	4	4	3	2	3	2
June	7	8	1	8	12	—
July	1	5	—	8	12	—
Aug.	2	7	—	5	13	—
Sept.	1	10	2	6	4	8
Oct.	2	3	5	5	4	8
Nov.	3	8	3	6	8	1
Dec.	8	5	—	5	6	2
Total:	34	56	23	49	65	24
Percent	30	49	21	36	47	17

1960

	Pravda		—	Izvestia		
Jan.	10	4	3	14	9	2
Feb.	3	2	—	6	6	1
Mar.	1	5	1	8	7	1
Apr.	1	3	—	8	8	—
May	34	—	5	27	1	—
June	24	3	1	23	2	1
July	15	1	—	24	3	—
Aug.	10	5	4	26	5	3
Sept.	12	2	3	17	3	5
Oct.	17	5	3	23	7	1
Nov.	12	2	4	25	3	2
Dec.	16	2	5	19	5	1
Total:	155	34	29	220	59	17
Percent	71	16	13	74	20	6

1961

	Pravda		—	Izvestia		
Jan.	7	9	3	9	7	—
Feb.	—	11	2	3	15	2
Mar.	2	6	3	10	11	2
Apr.	7	3	3	7	6	3
May	—	2	1	10	6	1
June	1	6	1	5	3	—
July	5	2	2	15	17	—
Aug.	7	8	18	14	11	3
Sept.	3	5	3	4	5	—
Oct.	3	10	7	7	5	1
Nov.	9	6	3	8	7	—
Dec.	7	4	5	7	12	—
Total:	51	72	51	99	105	12
Percent	29	42	29	46	49	6

1962

	Pravda		—	Izvestia		
Jan.	7	13	3	9	6	—
Feb.	7	5	4	13	5	—
Mar.	10	5	4	7	5	—
Apr.	11	1	4	10	2	—
May	7	10	—	7	4	—
June	12	3	—	12	5	1
July	6	2	6	9	6	1
Aug.	7	1	11	8	12	8
Sept.	2	1	—	13	12	—
Oct.	1	1	4	11	5	—
Nov.	—	1	2	—	9	3
Dec.	6	5	4	9	16	—
Total:	76	48	42	108	87	13
Percent	46	29	25	52	42	6

	1963 Pravda	—	Izvestia			1964 Pravda	—	Izvestia				
Jan.	1	4	2	13	9	—	7	4	—	17	19	1
Feb.	2	6	2	10	12	—	7	2	—	15	12	—
Mar	1	—	—	9	6	1	6	2	—	25	3	—
Apr.	—	1	3	3	1	—	—	2	—	10	3	—
May	6	—	1	14	2	—	2	3	1	8	5	1
June	—	1	5	4	6	5	7	5	1	9	6	3
July	1	—	1	8	5	—	6	—	—	16	5	—
Aug.	2	2	—	6	2	2[a]	—	—	—	15	4	—
Sept.	3	3	—	6	5	—	2	2	1	16	4	—
Oct.	1	1	—	6	9	—	5	2	1	11	8	2
Nov.	3	5	2	17	12	2	7	7	—	14	7	—
Dec.	3	3	4	7	6	—	12	8	—	20	6	—
Total:	23	26	20	103	75	10	61	37	4	176	82	7
Percent	33	38	29	55	40	5	60	37	3	65	33	2

[a] One of these cartoons was also favorable to the West.

CARTOON INDEX

TEXT INDEX